THE THAMES AND HUDSON MANUALS
GENERAL EDITOR: W. S. TAYLOR

Silversmithing

GW00578246

Frances Loyen

The Thames and Hudson
Manual of Silversmithing

with 176 illustrations

Thames and Hudson

Set, printed and bound in Great Britain by
Fakenham Press Limited, Fakenham, Norfolk

Contents

Part IV THE FINISHING PROCESSES

Acknowledgments

I wish to thank the Victoria and Albert Museum and the Worshipful Company of Goldsmiths for granting permission to reproduce photographs from their collections, and Susan Hare for the time and help she gave when choosing them. I would also like to thank the Sir John Cass School of Art for allowing me to photograph its students and tools.

Alix Sharkey gave his skill and many hours to working out and executing the workshop drawings, as did Laural Wade and Rick Eyres who took the documentary photographs. John Stoddard drew the technical illustrations, Elizabeth Duckworth read through the text with me, and Jane Townsend typed it. My thanks to them.

I am indebted to the following for their advice on various techniques: Arthur Withers (smallworking), Henry Pierce and Brian Fuller (spoon-making), Peter Gainsbury and B. A. C. (casting), Bernard Hulks (spinning), Brian Marlowe and David Simpson (polishing), and Anthony Elson on the workings of the trade.

The photographs from the Victoria and Albert Museum are on pages 1, 2, 51, 61 and 63; those from the Worshipful Company of Goldsmiths on pages 3, 36, 50, 70, 71 and 79. The tables on pages 182 and 183 are reproduced by kind permission of Johnson Matthey Metals Ltd.

F.L.

1 Gold granulated bowl. Etruscan, 5th–3rd century BC

2 Studley bowl, silver gilt. English, late 14th century

Introduction

The origins of silversmithing are lost in antiquity. Flourishing in Greece and later in Byzantium, this handicraft was encouraged by the medieval church. Workshops were set up in monasteries, though not all those engaged in this activity were necessarily monks. Gradually the craft began to develop outside the church and, because precious metal was a basic requirement, those involved often also acquired business acumen. Since the working properties of silver and gold are similar, for a long time the term 'goldsmith' was used for anyone working with either metal, although the work was always mainly done in silver. The word 'silversmith' only came into common usage very gradually, during the eighteenth century.

Goldsmiths in England formed a guild early in the twelfth century. One of the duties of the guild was to see that no gold or silver was sold anywhere in London except in the Cheap and the King's Exchange. It became a matter of paramount importance to ensure that the purity of these precious metals was controlled. A statute was enacted in 1300, introducing the practice of hallmarking, which was enhanced by another charter in 1462, entrusting the guild with the supervision of the craft throughout the country. Members of the guild, having access to a valuable commodity, began to take on roles as bankers and became generally influential. In 1327 the Worshipful Company of Goldsmiths was awarded a charter by Edward III.

In the later Middle Ages goldsmiths often held important civic positions – no less than seventeen acted as Lord Mayors of London before 1524. The fortunes of the guild fluctuated in the centuries that followed. The significant part that goldsmiths played in the development of banking in England came about almost by accident as the result of the peremptory act of Charles I in 1640 when he seized their precious metals, deposited in the Tower. Members of the guild then began to build their own strongrooms and this led to the storing of their clients' money from which the processes of banking naturally followed. Perhaps as the result of the growing importance of this work and the decline in the prestige of gold-

3 Taper candlestick with hammered
base. Richard Greene, 1714

smithing as a craft, the dual roles of goldsmith–banker
and goldsmith–craftsman began to become more distinct. But the craft itself has never lost its position among
the other decorative arts such as ceramic work and furni-
ture design.

Hallmarking of precious metal goods is still enforced
in the United Kingdom. Many other countries also have
regulations regarding the quality marks on gold, silver
and platinum work, but these are complex and variable.
The United States of America has a National Stamping
Act. It is illegal to offer for sale there an object of precious
metal with a quality mark unless the article also bears the
registered trade mark of maker or seller.

Silversmithing may be divided mainly into two
categories, largework, which consists of pieces that are
formed from sheet by being hammered or spun, among
which are coffee-pots, trophies and other sorts of
hollow-ware, and smallwork, which may have some
forming of the sheet metal, but is mostly concerned with
fitting and soldering together pieces of metal. This
includes boxes, watch-cases and ornaments generally.
Cutlery involves other processes.

A silversmith may be commissioned to do many
things, a unique article or perhaps a line of work such as a
goblet to commemorate some event. In this manual the
techniques required are clearly explained, from which it
will be seen that there is a difference in the approach to
making single pieces and to working in limited quan-

4 Silver goblets, tops and bases spun, stems cast, showing hallmarks. Anthony Elson, 1978

tities. The aim of the author is to help the student master the processes and to show a practising craftsman how to perfect his skills. This book does not deal with the decorative processes such as enamelling, repoussé work, chasing and engraving. Emphasis is laid on the constructional aspects of silversmithing which the reader is taken through, step by step in order of execution. Documentary photographs specially taken illustrate each stage. The book begins with detailed information and advice on how to set up a workshop, on the necessary tools and how to obtain these economically. There are suggestions as to how to correct mistakes and to avoid accidents which can happen when dealing with sharp instruments, hot metal and strong acids.

The importance of the initial design is stressed and one chapter is devoted to the subject of technical drawing. The working properties of precious metals are explained and conversion charts for ready reference are included in a useful set of appendices. The text is comprehensive and the explanations precise so that a craftsman following instructions should be able to produce a finished article with accuracy. The numerous illustrations include examples of work by some of today's outstanding practitioners, showing what may ultimately be achieved in this technically demanding and artistically creative craft where the basic skills have changed little, apart from the introduction of modern mechanical processes, since they were first used in ancient times.

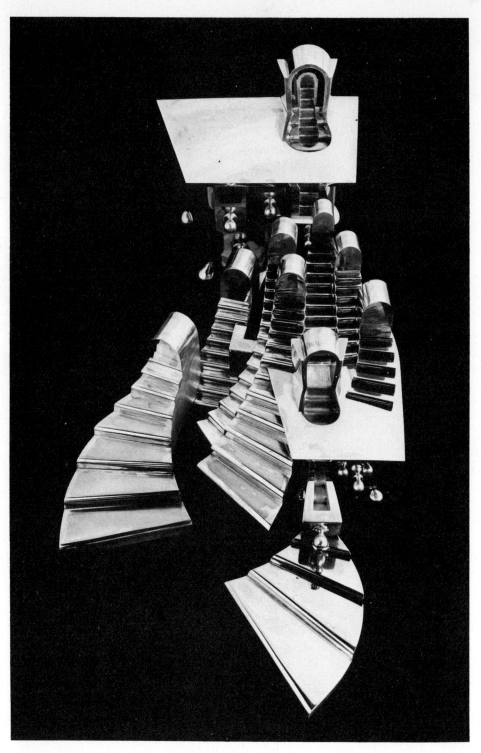

5 Sterling silver pomander, made using smallwork techniques, with drawers and containers for pot-pourri and essences. 20×30×50 cm. Michael Rowe, 1974

List of technical terms

Softening work-hardened metals which are heated until cherry red, then cooled by quenching (non-ferrous metal) or slow cooled (ferrous metal).
ANNEALING

Collar of sheet metal inside a box that holds the lid in place.
BEZEL

Measuring gauge. Also known as Shakespeare's Gauge.
BIRMINGHAM METAL GAUGE (BMG)

Highly polished metal finish.
'BLACK FINISH'

Sheet of metal that is to be worked.
BLANK

Flux used in hard-soldering.
BORAX

Doming up from the reverse side of a piece of metal.
BOSSING

Thickening the edge of a form during raising by striking the top edge with a hammer.
CAULKING

Tubing used to make hinges. Can be thin-wall or thick-wall.
CHENIER

Half-round wire bent in two for holding nuts in position, used by silversmiths for clamping work to be soldered or to support work on the soldering hearth.
COTTER-PIN

Metric measuring gauge.
DIXIÈME GAUGE

Stretching out, pulling down wire to a certain size.
DRAWING

Capable of being drawn into wire.
DUCTILE

Filing to a line; filing a piece of metal square.
FILING TRUE

Formation of an oxide just under the surface of standard silver and some carat golds, causing a dark stain.
FIRESTAIN

Substance for keeping surfaces clear of dirt and oxides during soldering.
FLUX

Alloy of nickel (does not contain silver).
GERMAN SILVER

Gold electro-plating (see Plating). Gold leaf is not used in this context.
GILDING

An alloy of zinc and copper, similar to brass.
GILDING-METAL

GRAVER	Small hand-held tool used by an engraver.
HEADS	Small formers used for raising and planishing metal.
INVESTMENT	Fast-drying mixture of plaster and silica in the form of quartz and cristobalite.
KNOCKING OUT	Hammering the flat base of a container on the inside to give it a curve.
KNUCKLES	Short pieces of chenier that make up a hinge.
LEMEL	Filings and scrapings of waste precious metals.
MALLEABLE	Capable of being hammered.
MANDREL	Large triblet; a straight, tapered steel stake.
MONEL	Alloy of nickel, very springy.
'... ON AIR'	Malleting, hammering or spinning 'on air': the main body of the work is supported but the part being worked stands free, and is forced down 'on air'.
PAILLON	Small piece of solder.
PEENING	Method of forming a shallow piece from a small, flat sheet of thick gauge.
PIANO WIRE	Hardened steel wire.
PICKLE	Acid solution used to clean non-ferrous metals after soldering and annealing, made up with sulphuric acid (1 part) and water (8 parts).
PIN	Piece of wood that projects from centre of work bench over the skin, against which work is held during filing and piercing.
PINK PORTHOS	Polishing compound.
PLANISHING	Smoothing metal by pinching it between a polished tool and hammer.
PLATING	Flattening a sheet of metal by annealing it between two flat steel plates. Also a term used for electro-plating, covering with a layer of metal by means of an electric current.
PUMICE	Abrasive used for the first stages of polishing.
QUENCHING	Cooling in water.
RAISING	Forming a flat sheet of metal into a vessel by hammering and compressing it to shape over a stake or former.
SAFETY-PICKLE	Sulphuric acid in crystal form.
SCORPER	Cutting tool used to carve metal.
SELVYT CLOTH	Soft flannel-like material.
SKIN	Leather skin fixed under work bench to collect lemel.
SOLDERING	Joining metals by fusing with an alloy.

Wire attached to a pattern that is to be cast. It forms the sprue hole, the opening down which molten metal is poured. — SPRUE

Filing a piece of metal each side square to the next, or with each lying at the correct angle. — SQUARING UP

Steel former used for raising metal. — STAKE

Tree-trunk with holes in to support stakes, and also with depressions in which to block metal (see Swage block). — STEADY

Two blocks of steel screwed together. This is used for forming decorative wire from either square or round section wire. — SWAGE

Rectangular block of steel into which D section grooves of varying widths and depths are cut. Used for hammering steel into sharp curves such as when making tubing. — SWAGE BLOCK

Steel block with cushioned edges, used for forming spoons. — TEIST

Pattern used as a guide when designing or checking work, and cutting metal. — TEMPLATE

Covering the face of a sand mould with soot to help the flow of silver during sand-casting. — TORCHING

Abrasive fine sand mixed with vegetable oil. — TRENT SAND

Small mandrel. — TRIBLET

Polishing compound. — TRIPOLI

Cutting a rotating piece of metal, wood, ivory or plastic. — TURNING

Soft slate sticks used for finishing metal, grinding away scratches. — WATER OF AYR STONE

Waterproof paper coated with silicone carbide or carborundum. — WET AND DRY PAPER

6 Work bench (with skin for collecting lemel), gas torch, bench hearth, vice and other tools

PART I:
BASIC REQUIREMENTS

1   The workshop

When first setting up a workshop the general order in which each part of a job is done should be thought out in advance. Careful planning within the limitations set by the size and shape of the room will allow articles to be produced more easily and efficiently.

Bench

This should be solid with a hardwood top such as beech and should have sturdy legs braced to the floor for stability. It can be made either as an individual bench or as a long one to seat several people. The top can be made from a wide single plank of wood, or by using lengths of wood in 5 cm sections that can be screwed together, the lengths being cut to the intended long dimension of the bench. A convenient way to begin is by attaching a 5 × 10 cm length, wide edge to the wall at bench height. Then similar lengths of 5 cm square section should be cut and placed alongside. When the first one has been drilled and screwed in place, the other 5 × 5 cm pieces should be dealt with similarly, holes being drilled and counter-sunk. The row of holes in each length should be bored out of line with those in the last one. As each length is drilled it is screwed and glued into the previous one. The number of holes in each length of wood obviously depends on the size of the bench, but they should be spaced at approximately 10 cm intervals. The 5 × 5 cm lengths (the bench top) are further supported by 5 × 5 cm lengths at each end, set at right angles to the wall, and by two legs, also 5 × 5 cm lengths, screwed to these at the front edge of the bench.

The ideal height for the bench is such as to allow the worker to sit at it, preferably using a chair rather than a stool, without having to bend his back too much or strain upwards, which can cause backache.

A semi-circular opening should be cut out of the front of the bench giving the craftsman a more convenient space in which to work. A movable wedge of wood, known as a 'pin', should project from the centre of the opening on which the piercing and filing can be done. This pin can be cut and filed, and used to support the work. A piece of leather should be hooked under the opening in the bench to catch the lemel, the precious metal waste that results from piercing and filing. This skin also serves to break the fall of a piece of silverware that might be dropped while being worked. It is helpful to have a small brush to sweep the metal filings from the bench into the skin and a magnet to pick out any bits of steel, such as broken sawblades. Lemel should be kept as clean as possible as it can be sold back to a bullion dealer at the current scrap price.

Some kind of vice is essential, and a small one bolted into the bench within easy reach of the work space is useful. If a lot of raising and hammering is to be done, it is sensible to have a leg vice as well which is fastened to the bench with an iron leg extending down to the floor and bolted to it, taking the strain from the bench and also from the jaws of the vice. If little raising is to be done, then an engineer's vice will be adequate.

Underneath the bench a gas tap should be fixed to take a blowtorch used for small soldering, which needs to be supported on top of the bench, possibly by means of a fixed, hooked piece of wire. A good source of lighting is required, the angle of which can be altered at will. In addition to the standard hearth used in the studio, there should be a small revolving bench hearth on the work top.

Hearth

The processes of soldering (joining metals by fusing with an alloy) and annealing (softening metals by heating to cherry red and cooling by quenching for non-ferrous metals and slow-cooling for ferrous metals) can be carried out either with natural gas and air from a compressor or by means of compressed gas. If the hearth is in a dark part of the workshop, the colour of the heat glow from the metal can be seen more clearly, thus making it easier to judge the temperature of the metal. The hearth itself should consist of a pan which is made from heavy iron or sheet steel. This can be bought new, perhaps found in a scrap-metal yard, or supplied by a firm dealing in second-hand machinery. Miscellaneous parts of machinery can often be adapted to make useful pieces of equipment.

A good size for the hearth is from 40 cm to 60 cm in diameter. It must be stable with a cast base, but also capable of revolving easily. It should be filled with pumice chips which are bought in lump form and broken up. Firebricks about 30 cm square are useful for supporting work that is being soldered. The tray should be surrounded by a frame of fireproof material, such as asbestos, to contain and equalize the heat that is essential for good soldering. The gas tap, torch and compressor should be next to the hearth. It is also useful to have handy insulated tweezers, borax, solder and steel tongs for carrying metal to the sink.

Pickle tank

The pickle or acid tank is used for cleaning the metal after annealing or soldering, and the best place to set it is next to the sink and near the hearth. It is usually a lead-lined tank which is heated on a gas-ring or fitted with an immersion heater. If the size of work usually done is not too large then a pyrex dish on an electric hot-plate can be used quite efficiently. A sink and pickle tank built into a bench is an ideal arrangement, but then care should be taken to ensure that the wood surrounding the pickle tank is painted with an acid-resistant paint or varnish. If acids are to be used regularly then the sink should be fitted with a neutralizing chamber. (More information about this can be obtained from the local authority.) Sulphuric acid, used for pickling the metal, should be diluted with water, in the ration of 1 to 8. (N.B. Always add the acid to the water, never the other way round.) A cupboard under the sink is useful for storing acids, together with sawdust and soda for neutralizing them. (Household soap will help to neutralize sulphuric acid spilt on clothes.) It is also necessary to have copper tongs to remove pieces of work from the pickle, as steel tongs react with the acid, causing a layer of copper to be transferred on to the precious metal. The pickle should be changed regularly. Care should be taken to ensure that the pickle never boils dry as the fumes given off are extremely dangerous. When the level of acid falls more water should be added to top it up; this can be done to diluted acid as long as the level is not too low, but never to concentrated acid.

Safety in the workshop

Organizing the workshop well helps a great deal to make it a safer place. Stakes and hammers that are stored in strong racks are less likely to crush one's toes than those left lying around. The floor should be swept regularly, kept clean and any grease or water mopped up immediately. Files should be put away after use and should always have handles – the tang is sharp and can easily slip, perhaps causing a nasty gash in an arm.

When using machinery, one should wear an overall and preferably heavy shoes, tie back loose hair and remove jewellery. It is a good idea also to wear goggles. Unfamiliar machinery should only be operated under supervision, and the stop button must be found before starting a machine. A workshop is full of potentially dangerous things – gas, flames, sharp tools, revolving parts on machinery, corrosive acids and various chemicals – all of which must be treated with respect. Pieces of work that are being polished should not be held in a cloth, since this can become entangled in the wheel, catching one's fingers.

An air extractor is an important part of a workshop as acids are in constant use. Acid itself should be put away, preferably next to a sink. A good first aid kit should be kept handy and acid burns washed immediately in running water: if they are serious, a doctor should be consulted.

2   The tools

The tools used fall into several categories – large machinery, hand machinery, forming tools, hammers, hand tools, measuring equipment and finishing products. Below follows a check list of essential tools; more detail is given in individual chapters.

LARGE MACHINERY

Lathe   To have both an engineer's lathe and a spinning lathe would be ideal, but most jobs can be fitted on to the latter, which is used for shaping a piece of work, with a wooden former on a rotating spindle and turning, i.e. cutting a rotating piece of metal. It is a useful piece of equipment, though not essential when starting a workshop, and can be bought second-hand.

Double-ended grinder   A machine useful for making tools, grinding shapes, etc. and essential for sharpening lathe tools, gravers, chisels. It can be bought second-hand.

Polishing motor   Essential for good polishing: the motor should run at 2800 rpm; if it is slower, polishing is much harder work. A guard and a cut-out switch should be within easy reach of the working position. An extractor fan makes polishing cleaner and less arduous. Second-hand motors are quite adequate.

HAND MACHINERY

Bench drill   A hand drill fixed on a stand will do some jobs, but the majority will need an accurate bench drill. A table that moves can be fitted to one for milling (horizontal cutting) purposes. Chuck jaws up to 12 mm are preferable and the drill should be bought new.

Draw-bench   This consists of a long narrow bench with a gap in its side along which a circular chain runs, to which

7 Draw-bench

a handle is attached. Wire, held by heavy iron drawtongs, (see p. 32) is pulled through a drawplate down to a different size section (see p. 106). A draw-bench generally has to be bought new. If a second-hand one is seen, it should be snapped up immediately.

Rolling mills   This hand-operated machine has two sets of rollers, one for wire and the other for sheet, which can be worked separately. It draws down square wire, making it smaller in section (see p. 104) and reduces the gauge of sheet. As it is rarely found second-hand, it has to be bought new.

Fly-press   This is a tool used to shape metal by stamping (see p. 131). It comes in various weights and sizes, depending on the job in hand. The dies have to be made up, simple ones being made in the workshop; more complex ones are sent out to a die-sinker. This is not essential equipment, and can be bought second-hand. It is useful in the production of a number of identical pieces.

Pendant drill   Driven by an electric pedal through a flexible shaft, it has an assortment of chucks into which heads on spindles fit, for use in small polishing, cutting, drilling and grinding.

Natural gas torch and *compressor* or *bottled gas*

FORMING TOOLS

Silversmiths' forming tools are known as stakes and heads, and are made from cast steel, the precious metal being hammered over them to form the required shape (see p. 139). The size and exact shape will depend on the work being done; some may be flatter on top than others, or have a more rounded nose. It is useful to collect bits of steel that can be filed or ground to shape; scrap-metal yards again can be a source for such items as axles, old railings, etc. Pieces of steel, brass, gilding-metal and aluminium always come in useful in the workshop for templates, dies and hand tools.

Steady A tree-trunk with depressions cut into it used for blocking is essential for carrying out the first stage of raising and for knocking out the bottoms of such vessels as bowls, forming the curve on the bottom of the bowl. It also has holes cut into it to take heavy stakes. When a raising has been blocked, it is necessary to sit down to continue the raising in order to get the right leverage needed to hammer it evenly, so the tree-trunk should be the right height for this.

Stakes These are heavier and larger than heads (see below), and are best made with a steel face welded to a wrought-iron shank, giving a hard polished surface on which to hammer, coupled with a shank with some give in it that absorbs the blows and stops the hammer from juddering, as it would on a harder tool. The shapes of the different stakes (several will be used on one job) vary according to the work, and should all be kept polished and in good condition; a dent in the stake will be transferred on to the precious metal during hammering. The stakes are supported in a vice or a steady block and have a rough-tapered square shank, as a round smooth shank would grip less well in the vice and slip down. Occasion-

8 Two steadies showing holes for heavy stakes and depression for blocking

ally they can be bought, but more often they are first made up in wood and then sent to be cast. Smaller ones can be forged from mild steel bars and welded together. If great care is taken of these tools, they need never wear out. Stakes that have been cast to order should be filed, rubbed with emery and then with an emery compound on a polishing motor before being brought up to a good polished surface.

Heads These tools are either clamped into a vice or slotted into a 'horse' or 'crank'. A horse is a piece of steel approximately 53 cm across with square slots at either end to take the shank of a head. The shank of the horse is tapered and square in section, and is either fitted into a steady or clamped into a vice. The crank is a similar piece of steel, but slightly smaller, that can be used only when clamped into a vice. They both have one offset end that enables a vessel to be raised with a mouth much smaller than its widest diameter. Heads vary in shape and size (the

9 Assorted large stakes

10 Assorted stakes, used in a vice

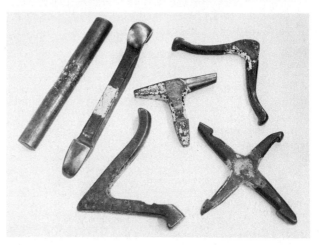

11 Horse and crank. Stake in centre can also be seen in Ill. 9

12 Heads used in the horse or crank. The two at the top are bottom stakes. *Lower right:* throw-back tool for raising, planishing, etc.

shanks are normally only 4 cm to 5 cm in length) and should be cared for in the same way as stakes. Bottom stakes are so called because they have shanks long enough to fit into the bottom of a deep vessel and are made in a variety of shapes and sizes.

Swage block A rectangular block of steel into which D-section grooves of varying widths and depths are cut. It is used for hammering sheet into sharp curves, usually when making tubing.

Doming blocks Cubes of steel or brass with a hemispherical recess into which the metal is forced with a ball-ended punch. They are made from either wood or steel and have a diameter ranging from 2 mm to 50 mm. Often the basic shape of a vessel can be formed on wood, the finishing stages being done on a metal tool, but the disadvantage of this method is that the shape of the vessel must be simple; the wood cannot be used more than a few times or it will split.

13 Doming block and punches

Mandrels Truncated cones, the larger ones being hollow, the smaller ones solid. They come in various lengths and degree of taper; some are free-standing and

14 Mandrels and a triblet. The largest mandrel has a wall thickness of 2 to 2.5 cm. The height varies from 20 to 50 cm

others have a short shaft that can be clamped into a vice. Mandrel is also the name for a parallel round steel bar, used for making napkin-rings and cylindrical boxes.

Triblets Small mandrels used for making rings. They also come in various sizes and degree of taper. Both mandrels and triblets are available in different sections, the most common being round and oval. They are also made in square and hexagonal sections. There is a round one with a groove cut in one side. All these tools have a machined, highly polished surface.

Among the forming tools it is necessary to have a flat stake. A surface plate should be kept on the bench, since this is essential for marking, measuring and checking for precision; but, as it is usually cast with an accurate machined finish, care must be taken not to hammer it too hard or it may crack or dent. A smaller steel block should be kept on the bench for hammering pieces flat or straightening wire, and an anvil with a machined finish should be kept in the workshop to use on larger work. When learning to use a hammer there is always a risk of damaging a flat surface. The half-moon dents that result from incorrect hammering can be filled from most stakes, but are difficult to remove from flat steel ones or from surface plates.

HAMMERS

Every stage in silversmithing requires a different hammer. Those used most often include:

Blocking A heavy hammer used on wood or a sandbag to start the first stages of raising; it comes in various shapes and sizes, ranging from full-faced to hemispherical. None of them has sharp corners. Weight approximately 1.5 kg.

15 Hammers, *left to right:* rawhide and two wooden mallets, blocking hammer, two raising hammers and a planishing hammer

16 Hammers, *left to right:* two collet hammers, setting hammer, bossing hammer for reaching inside tall narrow vessels, raising hammer and engineer's hammer

Forging   Heavy full-faced hammer used for forging silver for spoons and cutlery generally, or steel for making tools. Weight approximately 1.5 kg.

Raising   There are several shapes and sizes of raising hammer to suit different ways of working. The wide rectangular face reduces the likelihood of making half-moon cuts in the surface of the metal. The edges are cut away and softened, the face is flat and set at an angle from top to bottom edge. When used for raising, the top edge of the hammer strikes the metal and compresses it. Weights vary between 250 g and 300 g.

Planishing   The face on this hammer should be kept well polished and it should only be used for planishing, the smoothing out of metal and final stage of hammering. It has two faces, one square and the other round. Weights vary between 100 g and 200 g.

Bossing   This hammer is used for bossing or doming the work from the back and sinking the bottom of bowls. Weight approximately 200 g.

Collet   This hammer comes in various shapes and sizes, and is used for raising and planishing awkward concave shapes. Weights vary from 100 g to 250 g.

Setting   A large heavy hammer used for setting trays and other large flat surfaces. It has a flat face, well polished with softened corners. It is difficult to wield as it is heavy and, unless controlled properly, will dent the metal. This tendency can be overcome with practice. Weight approximately 1 kg.

Box   A small hammer about 2.5 cm square; it has two flat faces both with grooves cut out, one at the top of the face, the other at the bottom, to allow access to awkward corners or under the bezels of boxes. Weight approximately 100 g.

Engineer's   All-purpose hammer.

Riveting   This small hammer is used to flatten the ends of rivets. Also known as a 'toffee hammer'.

Mallets   Made from boxwood, rawhide or horn, these may be bought in several sizes. The corners of the boxwood mallet should be rounded with a rasp to prevent it from being spoilt by pieces splitting off. The face of a rawhide mallet should be broken in before use as it is covered with a hard coating of resin that chips off and can badly mark the precious metal being worked.

HAND TOOLS – CUTTING

Files   There are several different shapes, lengths and cuts of hand files. The most useful lengths are 15 cm to 20 cm. Below is a basic list of hand files needed:

Flat-pillar file	15 cm Cut 2
Half-round file	15 cm Cut 2
Sage-leaf file	15 cm Cut 2
Square file	15 cm Cut 2
Three-square file	15 cm Cut 2

Other useful files to have are a knife-edge, which has two flat sides with one edge wider than the other, a round one and a safety-back. The latter has only one cutting face. A 22 cm file, cut 0, should be used for filing steel only and a rasp kept for wood. Files for precious metals should be used solely for these and not for other metals such as steel, brass and aluminium. Gapping files may be cylindrical or flat with the half-round cutting faces on the two edges of the file. They are used for filing gaps to fit hinges and are necessary for box-making. A handle is fitted on to files by heating the file tang gently and burning it into the handle. It should then be removed quickly, quenched and pushed back in again firmly, the handle being banged sharply on a hard surface to jam the file in.

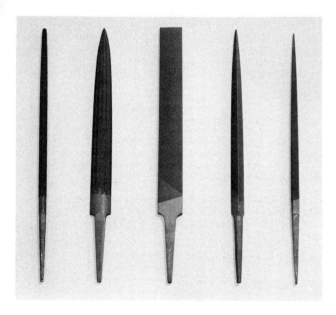

17 Hand files, *left to right:* round, half-round, flat or pillar, three-square and square

18 Assorted needle files

19 Rifflers

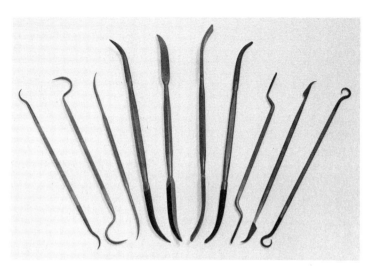

Needle files These are smaller than hand files (16 cm × 5 mm; the metal handle is included in this size). Flat, round, half-round, three-square, safety-back and knife-edge are all essential. They can be bought separately or in sets, both in medium and fine cut.

Rifflers Curved to file parts inaccessible to a straight file, rifflers are made for every shape imaginable and in several sizes. They are best bought just when the need for them arises.

Broaches Used for 'easing out' holes, making them slightly bigger where a drill would open them out too much, they are long thin five-sided pieces of steel, each side having a cutting edge. Made in a variety of sizes, used by smallworkers and jewellers, they should be bought only when needed.

Piercing sawframe This should have a solid frame and be well balanced. Adjustable sawframes can be bought, but tend to wear and do not give the stability needed for fine piercing. Blades are available from sizes 8/0 to 1/0 and up to No. 3. 8/0 is the finest. Useful sizes are No. 2 for cutting metal, 2/0 for slightly finer work and 6/0 to 8/0 for very fine piercing.

Backsaw This is used by smallworkers for cutting open boxes, when making the lid. It is important to buy a good quality backsaw with a straight blade which is a thin piece of steel with a serrated edge. It should be bought only if really needed.

20 *Top:* hacksaw; *centre:* two pairs of shears, a graver and a scorper; *bottom:* piercing sawframe

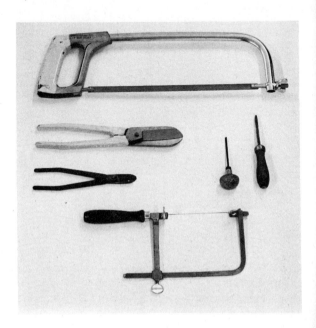

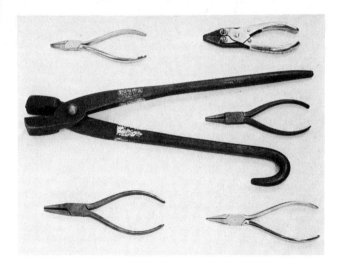

21 Pliers, *left to right from top:* in rows: *1* flat, *2* parallel, *3* large drawtongs, *4* round, *5* half round, *6* snipe-nosed

Hacksaw and blades Necessary for cutting steel when making tools.

Bench guillotine Useful for cutting large sheets of metal.

Shears Large hand-shears and a small pair for cutting wire and solder are both extremely useful, and it is essential to have at least one pair.

Taps and dies They should be bought only when needed, although it is slightly cheaper to buy them in sets.

Hand drill and drill-bits High-speed steel drills No. 1–60 metric size.

Gravers and scorpers Normally used by engravers for cutting and carving, but a square graver and two or three scorpers are necessary for cleaning solder out of awkward spots and making 'stitches' – small points of metal cut out of the surface of the job being worked to help hold it in position when soldering.

Scraper A three-sided cutting tool used to scrape the surface of metal to clean it, usually before soldering.

Scriber Used to cut a line into the surface of the metal when drawing in a shape or marking out measurements. It is an essential piece of equipment.

Oil-stones There are several stones that can be bought for sharpening tools. Carborundum stones are usually double-sided, fine and medium grade. Arkansas stones are better quality and last much longer; they are generally mounted in a wooden box. It is important to keep tools sharp and so some sort of oil-stone is necessary. A piece

31

of equipment called an 'edge tool honer' can be bought which holds the tool firmly at an angle when it is being sharpened.

Pliers　The name of each type of pliers describes the shape of its head. It is necessary to have a small selection of pliers. Parallel pliers or slide tongs are for holding the work, flat, half-round and snipe-nosed for bending and shaping the metal. Tool-makers' clamps are useful for holding metal and also for clamping pieces of metal together to file or to pierce them into the same shape.

Ingot mould　This is a cast-iron mould made up of channels into which molten metal is poured.

Crucible　This is a container in which metal is melted; different crucibles should be used for different metals.

Tongs　Short, heavy tongs are used for lifting hot crucibles after melting metal.

Drawtongs　These are heavy iron tongs with serrated faces in the jaws to grip wire when it is being drawn down to size.

Other tools for holding metal are brass and steel tweezers, a set of pin vices, G-clamps and a joint tool (joint-leveller) used for holding tubing while it is being cut or filed and for holding wire when the end is being filed flat.

Centre-punch　An automatic centre-punch is used by pressing the tool with one hand; this makes a slight dent which is used to locate a drill-bit when drilling holes. An ordinary centre-punch will need two hands as it has to be hammered into the metal.

Burnisher　This is a highly polished steel tool, also made from agate or haematite, used to polish metal by compressing and burnishing.

HAND TOOLS – MEASURING

Miscellaneous

15 cm and 30 cm rulers, metal.
An engineer's square for measuring right angles.
Dixième gauge for gauging the thickness of metal.
Vernier gauge.
Spring-dividers – one large pair and one pair of tool-maker's dividers.
Callipers, inside and outside.
Micrometer. This is generally useful, especially for smallworking.

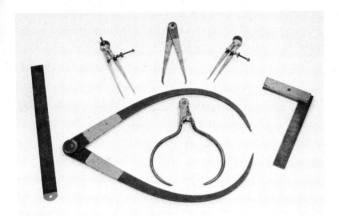

22 Measuring tools: ruler, outside callipers, inside callipers, dividers and engineer's square

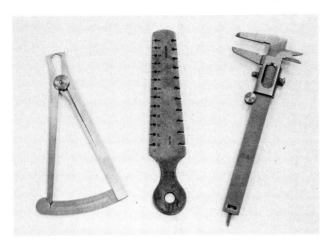

23 Measuring tools: dixième gauge, Birmingham Metal Gauge (BMG), vernier gauge

Pencil compasses These should be workshop compasses, not expensive drawing instruments.

Surface gauge Used on a surface plate to measure height and accuracy of work.

Surface plate Machined, case flat block for testing accuracy of work.

HAND TOOLS AND MATERIALS – FINISHING

Polishing equipment

Boxwood shavings for drying work without scratching it.
Brushes, brass, for cleaning the inside and outside of silverware.
Brushes, hand, hard bristle for scouring and cleaning, soft for cleaning off polish.

Burnisher.

Emery cloth for cleaning stakes and other tools.

Emery compound for polishing steel stakes.

Emery paper.

Mops, various. Rope mop for cleaning tools, calico hard, calico soft, swansdown, wool and felt mops. All these are used for polishing the outside of silverware. Bristle 'Turk's head' and other bristle mops, felt and wool mops for the inside of silverware.

Nylon scouring cloth.

Pumice powder.

Radio rouge, rouge, rouge powder. Finer polishing compounds; radio rouge is coarser than powdered rouge which is used for the final finish.

Trent sand, a fine sand mixed with vegetable oil. Very abrasive.

Tripoli and pink porthos. Both are polishing compounds, the former used for silver and brass, the latter for silver, gold and steel.

Waterproof silicone paper, known as 'wet and dry'. Grades 100, 180, 240, 320, 400, 500, 600.

Whiting powder.

Soldering equipment

Binding wire.

Borax, borax tray and brush.

Charcoal block, wig, wire grid. All are used to support work while it is being soldered.

Cotter-pins for holding together pieces of precious metal that are being soldered, or for balancing metal while soldering.

'Easy-flo' flux, a protective soft paste,

Solders, hard, medium, easy and extra easy.

Steel tweezers.

Miscellaneous

Acids, nitric and sulphuric. The latter can be bought as safety-pickle, a crystal form of the acid, making it easier to handle but no less dangerous when in use. Alum powder is a good, safe substitute for sulphuric acid for pickling so long as it is kept hot.

Lead cake, pitch, setter's wax, blocks of wood; all are useful for holding metal while it is being worked.

Machine oil (mineral oil).

Methylated spirits. Useful for cleaning off setter's wax, and for polishing.

Nickel wire for hinges.

Paraffin for cleaning pitch from metal.

Piano wire for hinges and drilling out inaccessible holes.

Sheet iron, 3 mm thick. Used for 'plating', a method of flattening or straightening sides of boxes.

Care of tools

When first setting up the workshop, it is worth buying good tools; they will wear out less quickly than cheap ones, and the finish on them will not affect the quality of the work being produced. A badly made pair of pliers or a stake with a hammer mark on it will transfer its imperfections on to the metal being worked. Care is essential for a high standard of craftsmanship. Stakes and hammers should be kept clean and oiled when not in use: the brighter the finish on a planishing hammer and a stake, the less the work that will have to be done when a piece reaches the polishing stage. Silversmithing hammers should be used only for working with precious metals, not for nails and other household jobs.

Racks can easily be made for stakes and hand files, and even needle files can be pushed into holes drilled in a block of wood. A wire brush should be kept to clean files. Any files that have wax on their cutting face should be warmed gently and brushed with the wire brush. Aluminium shields should be put in a vice before clamping in a stake or other tool, thus stopping the vice from passing on the imprint of the teeth on its jaws. Tightening screws on tools, such as the wing-nut on a sawframe, should not be done with pliers as the thread would eventually be worn. Measuring tools must never be hammered, dropped or clamped in a vice, since this affects their accuracy. Any tools that get wet will rust or be affected in some way; before further work is carried out all articles must be carefully dried after annealing.

Piano wire, a hardened steel wire, will blunt shears and cut grooves into rolling mills; this wire should either be snapped off or ground if a short length is needed.

Polishing mops will pass on the compound that has been used on them unless they are stored separately; even a fragment of coarse compound on a fine mop will take the finishing process back several stages. When mops are dirty they can be cleaned in washing-up liquid, ammonia and hot water, and soaked over-night.

3   Tool-making and working properties of metals used

Certain tools can be made in the workshop. The most obvious choice of metal is steel, which is available in different forms depending on its chemical make-up. It is made by blowing oxygen through molten pig-iron: various types of steel are produced by controlling the carbon content. Elements such as manganese, vanadium, nickel or tungsten may be added to produce types of steel with different characteristics.

Mild steel

This is the common, all-purpose steel. It comes in two forms: black or bright drawn steel. Black mild steel is cheaper, but is bought in less accurate dimensions, and working it is harder because of the black casing which tends to blunt the teeth of a file when being used. The black coating protects it to some extent from rust.

Bright drawn steel

The same metal as mild steel, with an accurate, machined, bright steel finish. It comes in exact sizes and is covered with oil as protection from the atmosphere. It lends itself to all workshop techniques, such as forging, filing, sawing, drilling and machining, and is used most often for making nuts, bolts, screws and nails. These steels can be properly hardened only by the addition of surface carbon (see below, *Case-hardening*). They are called low-carbon steels.

24 Steel box fired with gold. Malcolm Appleby, 1969

Cast steel

A high-carbon steel, it is supplied like mild steel with a black surface oxide. It can be forged and is the steel used for all metal-working tools. It can be hardened and tempered, but the cost is double that of mild steel.

Silver steel

Cast steel ground to accurate sizes and a bright finish; it is useful for tool-making when hardened steel of precise size is required.

High-speed steel

The name given to a group of steels containing ingredients such as tungsten and manganese, usually coloured dark blue, and marked H.S.S. The special property of high-speed steel is that when brought to red heat and allowed to cool slowly it will become hard: tools made from it cannot be softened and so can do work that would take the temper from another tool. Sawblades made from it are more brittle than other types of blades, but they can cut harder materials and will wear longer. It is often used for making drills.

Metal	Percentage of other element present apart from iron
Cast iron	3.5 per cent carbon. Too hard; cannot be worked.
Wrought iron	0.02 per cent carbon. Too soft for tools. Good for binding wire.
Mild steel	0.15–0.25 per cent carbon. Cannot be hardened and tempered properly, only case-hardened.
Cast steel	1.05–1.20 per cent carbon. Good for tool-making. Can be hardened and tempered.
High-speed steel	12–22 per cent tungsten. 2–6 per cent chromium. 3–5 per cent vanadium. Also cobalt and manganese.

Making a spear drill

Piano wire or a needle may be used, although the latter is not so hard. A carborundum stone is used in the same way as a file to take off the end of the wire square to the sides and to form the angles for the bit. Two angles are filed with the stone on to the wire opposite each other as on a screwdriver. The wire is then rested firmly against the pin and the corner of one of these angles is filed off. The wire is then turned over and the same is done to the other side, on the opposite corner.

Making a scoring tool

This is a cutting tool used by hand to score an angle into a piece of metal. The metal is then folded and soldered, so reproducing the angle that is on the tool. The angle at the tip of the tool varies, depending on the piece of work to be done. The easiest way to make a scoring tool is out of the tang of an old file. The metal must be annealed, that is to say heated, from half way up its length, and then allowed to cool. A hook has now to be put on the tool and shaped to the required angle.

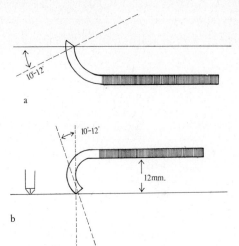

25 Angles to be filed on to a scoring tool

The tool when finished is used by pulling it along a scribed line, the angle at the end of the hook cutting into the metal. Using a forging hammer the tang of the file should be bent round the pointed end of the anvil to form a semi-circle. A template should now be made from aluminium. Mark the base line, the 90° point and the required angle, and join the marks on the paper, giving the angle needed. Trace on to a piece of aluminium that has previously been warmed and rubbed with wax: the mark left on the aluminium should be pierced out leaving a template of the required angle. The size of the piece of aluminium used need not be more than 1.5 cm square.

The tip should be annealed and filed back, the tool first being clamped in a vice. One should remember that the tool is to be pulled flat along a piece of metal. The curve must be wide enough to allow the tool to be held without the hand getting in the way. Then the angle on the tool should be filed, using the template as a guide. This angle must slope back, allowing only the front tip to come into contact with the metal it will be cutting. The tip is the cutting edge. The next stage is described below.

Hardening and tempering

When steel with a high carbon content is heated to a bright cherry red and quenched, it becomes glass-hard and brittle. For the quenching to be fully effective, the steel should be moved to and fro to release any steam bubbles on the surface of the metal which may check the sudden drop in temperature needed to make the metal hard. Tools quenched in oil are slightly softer, but tougher than those quenched in water. Once the tool is hard it should be tempered so that it will not crack when being used. The temper it is given depends on the job it is to be used for. (See next page.) The hardened steel should first be rubbed with emery paper to clean off any dirt or oxide on its surface, and then heated from half way down its length. This makes the body of the tool softer, which is necessary if a tool is to be struck, in order to absorb the blow and prevent the tool from bouncing. The clean metal will clearly show the colour, the oxide forming on the surface of the metal, climbing up the tool. When the correct colour has reached the tip of the tool it should be quenched. If a tool that has been hardened needs to be reworked, it should be annealed (remembering to allow the metal to cool slowly). However, if the metal is hardened and annealed too often, damage can be done to its texture, making it unworkable.

TEMPERING CHART

Colour	Degrees C	Tool
Dark blue	300°	Fine sawblades, springs, screwdrivers.
Purple	270–75°	Press tools, chisels, sawblades, wood-turning tools.
Red-brown	255–60°	Drills, shears.
Dark straw	240–45°	Hammers, chasing tools, taps, dies.
Light straw	220–30°	Scrapers, gravers, metal-turning tools, dividers.

Case-hardening

Because mild steel is low in carbon it does not respond to ordinary hardening techniques and therefore should be case-hardened. There are several ways of doing this. The tool can be packed in a sealed box with a meat bone, heated and then quenched, or the tool itself can be heated, drawn across a bone and quenched. This burns the bone, leaving a layer of carbon on the surface of the metal. Another way is to use case-hardening powder containing ferrocyanide and to coat the hot tool in this before quenching. The fumes given off when using this method, however, are dangerous and great care must be taken. When sharp tools such as chisels are being tempered it is difficult to give them a uniform heat, but it can be done in a kiln with a pyrometer attached, or if there is not one available, a box filled with sand containing the tool can be heated on a gas-ring until the correct temperature is reached. The tool should then be removed and quenched.

Hardening and tempering steel make it into a better cutting or hammering tool because the metal is given a hard finish while the tempering takes away the brittleness, making it fibrous and tougher.

Other non-precious metals

Apart from the different types of steel, there are several other metals used in the workshop. Brass can be used for making punches and dies, providing the tools are used with care; no heavy raising should be done on a brass stake. Its colour is pale to red-yellow, depending on the alloy used, this being a mixture of copper and zinc. It is harder than silver to file, but much softer than steel, and takes a dull oxide when exposed to the air. Brazing brass, an alloy of copper, zinc and lead, is useful for brazing iron, mild steel or brass when making tools.

Gilding-metal is similar to brass, being another alloy of copper and zinc. The working properties, however, are much nearer to those of silver, although it is slightly harder and tougher. It is used for making vessels that are to be silver-plated.

Copper, an element, also has working properties similar to those of silver, although when being raised it tends to compress more. If a base metal replica of a silver vessel is being made it is better to used gilding-metal than copper. The melting point of copper is 1083° C, specific gravity 8.96.

Nickel and alloys using nickel such as German silver are also used for making hollow-ware and jewellery. Nickel silver does not actually contain silver; the name refers only to its colour. Its working properties are similar to those of silver but it is harder to work, and needs to be annealed more often. It has to be carefully cleaned before soldering, as do copper and gilding-metal. Monel, another alloy of nickel, is particularly good for making springs in boxes and clasps.

Lead and aluminium are also useful in the workshop, but the filings from these metals must be removed from the bench or, better still, should never be allowed on the bench. Files for them should be kept separately, and remains swept from the hearth. A filing of either of these metals on a piece of silver or gold that is being annealed will immediately burn into the surface of the precious metal and, unless it is scraped off, will burn a hole in subsequent annealings. Aluminium faces should be put in the vice to protect the tool or vessel being worked on. Aluminium can also be used for setting hallmarks (the aluminium is planished over the hallmark, the job being supported on a well-fitting tool) and for templates. The softness of lead enables it to be easily punched into shapes, into which silver can be hammered. Scrap lead should be melted and poured into an old biscuit tin and, when this has dried, the tin should be cut away leaving a lead 'cake'. The required shapes are punched into this. Before the precious metal is worked a thin piece of paper should be put into the lead shape to protect the metal from the lead.

26 Patinated copper and
silver pomander.
58.42×30.48×22.86 cm.
Michael Rowe, 1971

Three refractory metals, niobium, tantalum and titanium, initially employed in the manufacture of surgical
instruments and implants, parts of guided missiles and air-
craft, have become popular among craft-workers though
they are used more by jewellers than silversmiths because
of the limitations of their working properties. The attraction of these metals lies in the fact that they can be
beautifully coloured by anodic oxidization, a method of
running an electric current through the metal to colour it,
the colour and shade depending on the voltage applied.
They cannot be cast or soldered under normal workshop
conditions, but can be joined by riveting or by using
adhesives. Titanium is virtually unworkable, apart from
simple forming operations such as bending, so it is
mainly used as a flat sheet. Niobium and tantalum can be
worked by raising, chasing or spinning but cannot be
annealed under ordinary working conditions. Designs
for pieces of work to be made in these metals must not be
too complicated. Both are more expensive than silver,
niobium being the harder and lighter of the two.

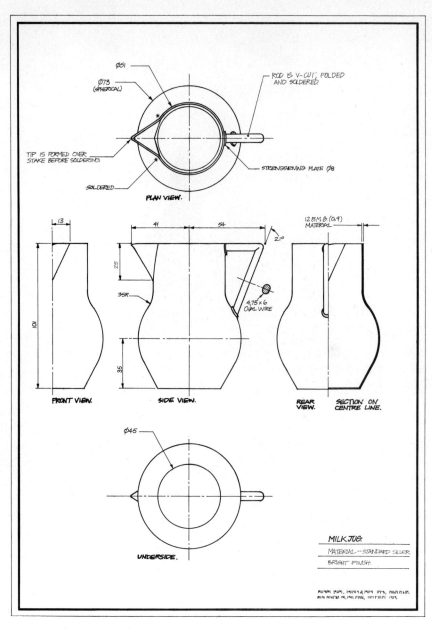

Ø51

Ø73
(SPHERICAL)

ROD IS V-CUT, FOLDED
AND SOLDERED.

TIP IS FORMED OVER
STAKE BEFORE SOLDERING.

STRENGTHENING PLATE Ø8

SOLDERED

PLAN VIEW.

13

41   54

2.10

12 B.M.G. (0.9)
MATERIAL

25

35R

4.75 x 6
OVAL WIRE

101

35

FRONT VIEW.   SIDE VIEW.   REAR
VIEW.

SECTION ON
CENTRE LINE.

Ø45

UNDERSIDE.

MILK JUG.

MATERIAL — STANDARD SILVER

BRIGHT FINISH.

27 Working drawing for a milk jug

4 Technical drawing

A basic knowledge is all that is required in a workshop but the drawings should be as clear as possible or they may be wrongly interpreted. A working drawing is often used when a silversmith designing a piece is not making it personally, or if the piece is complicated to make. A drawing is also used for working out details in smallwork such as the placing of a hinge or the development of a box. Preliminary drawings are important when planning a commissioned line of work where the price agreed dictates the way it will be made.

Little equipment is needed. A drawing board with a parallel motion is helpful, but it is expensive and a luxury unless it is to be used continually. A simple drawing board that can be set up at an angle is a good alternative. An adjustable set square, ruler and pencil compasses are required, as well as pencils, tracing-paper and a rubber. French curves (flexible perspex templates) can be bought to help draw curved lines accurately, but they should only be used after the design has been worked out carefully and is being drawn up. It is easy to stray from the original design when following the curve of a template.

Once the piece has been designed, it should be drawn up as a side view; most of the plan view and other side elevations can be taken from this. The centre line of the job is drawn in with a ruler or set square as a broken line, and a base line is drawn at right angles to it. From these points the other measurements such as height, width and the overall form are drawn in, giving a simple line drawing of the side view. If the two sides of the piece are identical, the first one can be drawn in and the measurements transferred with pencil compasses to the other, the outline being drawn in free hand or transferred with tracing-paper (Fig. 27).

The centre line is extended beyond the top and bottom of the job in order to draw the plan view above it and the underside below. For the plan the widest diameter and then the other diameters are measured from the centre line of the side view and transferred with pencil compasses to a point along the centre line above the side

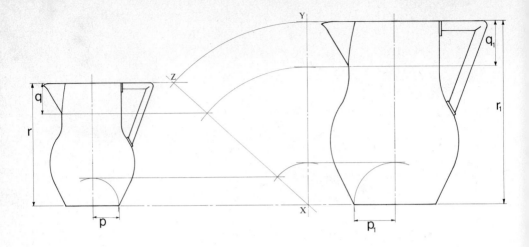

28 Enlarging to scale

view. Other parts such as the handle and spout in Fig. 27 are drawn in on the plan view by tracing a line parallel to the centre line on the side view and extending it as shown. The underside is done in the same way along the centre line at a point below the side view.

Once the side and plan views have been drawn, the front and rear views are added. In the front view on Fig. 27 the spout is the only detail and half of the form is drawn in, the other half being identical. Half the width of the spout is shown, the size being taken from the plan view. The height is also shown in measurements on this view. The rear view shows the handle, the width being taken from the plan, and the section is also shown on this part along the centre line. Half the spout and the thickness of metal used are drawn in. Unless specified elsewhere on the drawing G*12 (0.90 mm) is used to make the whole piece. Dimensions are indicated by arrowed lines.

All information on a working drawing should be kept to the minimum needed to define the piece. More can lead to confusion, and if one measurement is changed that should also be written down somewhere else as one may forget to change that second figure. A tracing should be made of the working drawing so that dyeline prints can be taken to give to out-workers. The measurements should be drawn in at the appropriate points (ø means diameter), and also information such as the size of the strengthening plate, the fact that the wire is oval and the rod V-cut folded and soldered. Once the drawing has been done it is a good idea to check back by imagining how one would make the piece, and then running through the drawing. A useful book on this subject is published by the British Standards Institution B.S. 308. Parts I and II, on General Principles and on Dimensioning and Tolerancing of Size are of particular interest.

If the thickness of the metal is to vary, such as having a thick top edge on a beaker, this should be drawn in

44

* BMG = Birmingham Metal Gauge.

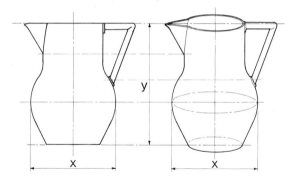

29 Relating a side elevation to a perspective view

carefully on the working drawing. The shapes of wires are also drawn in to show that they are separate from the main body of the piece and that they have been soldered on. If any details are too small to show on the drawing, or confuse it, they should be enlarged and shown separately.

Enlarging to scale

If it is necessary to enlarge a whole drawing to scale first draw the view to be enlarged (Fig. 28). The base line is extended and a new height line drawn xy. Resting compasses on x, swing down the new height to intersect the original height at point z. Draw in line zx. Some distance along the base line from the new height line xy the centre line of the enlarged piece is drawn. The height is transferred along from xy to the centre line. The height of features can be transferred along to zx and swung around to the new height q along to qi. Widths are enlarged by being swung on to the original centre line, using compasses, then drawing along to zx, swung to the new centre line, then down to the horizontal p to pi. The new height of every feature, curve, etc. must be found before the width. (The compasses are swung down to the new horizontal.)

Relating a side elevation to a perspective view

A side view can easily be drawn apparently in perspective by the use of a simple grid. (The resulting diagram, Fig. 29, is not in true perspective: it is a diagramatic version.) The side view is drawn, and then the base and height lines are drawn across to the new centre line. All the points on the vertical plane are drawn by transferring the widths across and marking them with compasses on the *correct* vertical line. The circles that are seen as horizontal lines in the side elevation are then tipped to form ellipses (being bisected by the top and base lines and the centre line). The ellipses (circles at top and base line seen in perspective) should not be too deep, for if tipped too much a distorted view of the piece will be seen. This is not a precise method of transferring a design but it is a good way of showing what a piece looks like in the round. Certain details, such as the strengthening plates on Fig. 29, require some personal interpretation when being drawn in. The method can also be used to transfer a perspective view into a side view.

Ellipses

Perspex ellipse templates of all sizes can be bought, but prove expensive unless they are to be used often, and it is more practical to draw without them. The circle is one of the most difficult of all shapes to draw in perspective. It is only when one is at right angles to the centre of vision, a plan view, that it is seen as a true circle; it is seen as a straight line if it is at right angles to the picture plane and parallel to the centre line of vision; if it is moved in any direction which changes its angle it becomes an ellipse.

An ellipse is an oval constructed on unequal axes which cross each other at right angles. When these axes are drawn in, it can be seen that the ellipse is made up of four identical quadrants which can be fitted into a rectangle. There are several ways of drawing an ellipse, the most straightforward one being to draw the major and minor axes inside a rectangle. With practice each quadrant can then be drawn in free hand. Another method is to draw the first quadrant, trace it, and transfer it to the other three sections (Fig. 30).

Because it cuts out construction lines and is more accurate, the trammel method is often used (Fig. 31). The major and minor axes are set up and a narrow strip of cardboard cut slightly longer than half that of the major axis. Point *a* should be marked at one end of the strip and, placing it at one end of the major axis, half the length of

30 Drawing an ellipse

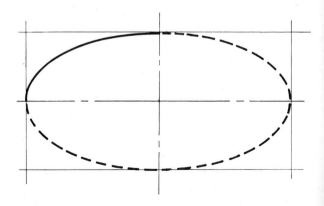

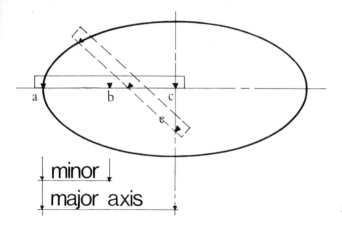

minor

major axis

31 The trammel method

the axis should be marked on the card as point *b*. The card is now placed on the minor axis, point *a* being lined up with the end of the axis. Point *c* is marked at the half-way point along the minor axis. The resulting strip with the three points marked on it is now placed across the two axes, point *c* resting on the major axis, point *b* on the minor. By keeping *b* and *c* constant at some point on the major and minor axes, but moving point *a*, an ellipse is formed. As the trammel is moved points are marked with a pencil at point *a*, mapping out the ellipse, which can later be joined free hand. If the major axis is so much longer than the minor axis that when the trammel is placed along it, point *b* stretches below the over-all length of the minor axis, then the line of this axis should be lengthened by a dotted line which acts as a guide-line for the trammel to follow.

Calculating a blank for a complex form

For a form such as a spout, a model should be made in clay, wax or plasticine. A template is taken from the side view of the drawing and the model built up in the medium preferred. The model can also be carved from wood or plaster. Making the model, which is a three-dimensional projection of the drawing, helps in working out the design, to see if the handle or spout is at the right angle, if the spout pours, and so on. The principle used to work out an irregular blank can be applied to most irregular forms such as cigar cases and ribbed boxes.

To make a D-section spout, that is a spout made up from two sheets of metal, one, a flat sheet, is soldered to the other, an elongated half-round, when it is has been shaped. The flat sheet can easily be calculated when the curved section has been made.

A full-size development of the spout can be sketched out. First the centre line of the spout is drawn on a piece of paper; using the template, the centre line is found on the model; it will be the point at which it fits the model on its

47

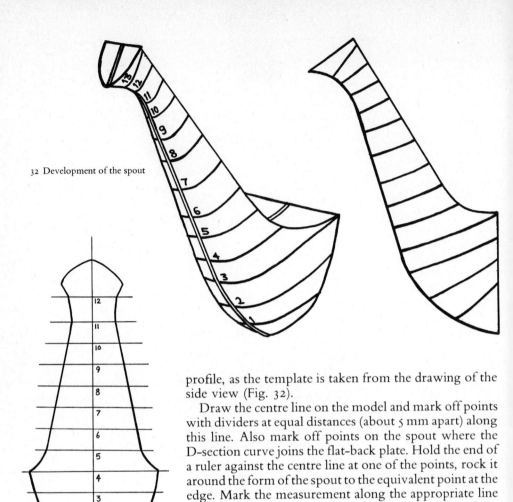

32 Development of the spout

33 Marking off measuring points on the model

profile, as the template is taken from the drawing of the side view (Fig. 32).

Draw the centre line on the model and mark off points with dividers at equal distances (about 5 mm apart) along this line. Also mark off points on the spout where the D-section curve joins the flat-back plate. Hold the end of a ruler against the centre line at one of the points, rock it around the form of the spout to the equivalent point at the edge. Mark the measurement along the appropriate line on the paper from the centre line. If both sides of the spout, on either side of the centre line, are the same the measurement should be marked on both sides of that line. Continue until the lengths of all of the lines joining the points have been measured, and then draw in the outline of the spout free-hand. This drawing can now be transferred on to the precious metal with tracing paper and pierced out (Fig. 33).

Calculating a blank for seaming

Seaming can be used to produce forms of any shape and size. Cylinders, such as are used to make round boxes, are easy to calculate: the diameter is multiplied by π (3.14 or $3\frac{1}{7}$) and the height is measured. Cones are used for many types of work that need to be seamed, raised or stretched, such as coffee-pots, vases, and so on. The diagram explains how to develop a cone into a flat sheet (Fig. 34).

When the piece has been drawn side view (see p. 73). the size of the cone is decided and should be drawn out as follows: *abcd* represents the cone. Extend *ab* and *cd* to meet at *e*. With *e* as the centre and radius *ea*, draw the arc through *c*, extending it past both points. With the centre *e* and radius *eb*, draw the arc through *bd*, and beyond on either side. Set compasses to the length of line *bd*, and using B as the centre, cut the arc beyond *b* at *i*. Repeat using *d* as centre, cutting the arc at *g*. Join *ie* and *ge*. *higf* represents the correct blank.

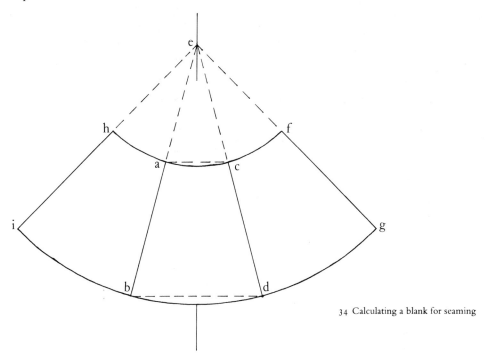

34 Calculating a blank for seaming

35 Raised cup. The first piece to be given a platinum hallmark. Jocelyn Burton, 1975

PART II: THE ARTICLES AND HOW TO MAKE THEM

5 Hallmarking and the working properties of precious metals

Hallmarking was first introduced in England in 1300 as a standard method of controlling the purity of silver and gold. It consists of a set of marks which is stamped on to all articles made in these precious metals (since January 1975 also platinum) to be sold in the United Kingdom after being tested or 'assayed'. Any manufacturer wishing to sell work made from these materials must be registered with an assay office which then issues him with a personal punch. This can be made either with his own initial or that of the company to which he belongs and it has to be stamped on to the main body of every piece presented to an assay office for hallmarking. No piece may be submitted unless it is complete apart from polishing. If a piece to be marked is made up of two different qualities of metal, e.g. standard silver and Britannia silver, then it will be punched with the mark of the lower standard.

The hallmark is made up of four parts: the maker's mark, the standard mark, the town mark of the assay office and the date letter. The standard mark guarantees the quality of the silver (which may be above that indicated by the mark); the town mark or assay office mark denotes the town where the piece is marked and the date letter the year when it was made. This letter is changed every year. Every twenty years a new cycle of letters is started with a different character and a different shield.

36 Modern hallmark on silver showing a maker's mark, sterling standard mark (lion), assay office mark (leopard's head for London), and date letter (1964)

The letters run from A–U, omitting J. At one time there were assay offices all over the United Kingdon, each starting the date letter at a different time, so it was necessary to know where it was stamped before being able to identify the date. From 1 January 1975 this was changed when all offices started to use the same letter. Many assay offices have now been closed down and there are just four today: London, Birmingham, Sheffield and Edinburgh. The one in Dublin is recognized only by marks struck before 1923. Knowing the date and which assay office was used to mark a piece of work is important because it means that the officers of the Goldsmiths' Company responsible for the assay can be traced.

Other marks have been added to the regular hallmark from time to time, for special purposes or occasions. From 1784 to 1890 a stamp of the sovereign's head had to be included, to show that a duty had been paid (collected by the assay office, the amount depending on the weight of the article). This mark, the heads of George III, George IV, William IV and Victoria in turn, is found at the appropriate dates. Three other marks have also been struck voluntarily by the assay office: the two heads of George V and Queen Mary to commemorate their Silver Jubilee in 1935, the head of Queen Elizabeth II in 1953 to commemorate her coronation, and in 1977 in celebration of her Silver Jubilee.

Once a piece has been submitted to an assay office in its rough form it is weighed. It is also weighed before being dispatched after hallmarking. The maker must state what type of metal and what standard he expects it to be before it is tested. If it does not come up to the right standard, the assay office is entitled to destroy the piece. However, if it comes up to a lower but still recognized standard then the assay office will mark it lower, e.g. an 18 carat gold object that is submitted but only comes up to the standard of 14 carat will be marked 14 carat.

The metals marked at the assay office and their percentage of precious metal per thousand parts are as follows:

Gold	22 carat	(916.6)
	18 carat	(750)
	14 carat	(585)
	9 carat	(375)
Silver	Britannia	(958.4)
	Sterling	(925)
Platinum	–	(950)

The piece of work is first scraped. This is done methodically, taking scrapings from the main body from any parts that have been soldered on to it and from those that are a part of the complete piece, such as a lid on a tea-pot. An exact weight of metal is taken for the sample to be assayed. There are different ways of testing gold, silver and platinum.

After the gold sample has been weighed, it is wrapped in a piece of lead foil, together with a sample of pure silver two and a half times the weight of the gold. This package is then placed in a magnesia crucible and melted in a muffle furnace at 1100°C. The lead oxidizes at this temperature and the oxide is absorbed into the crucible along with any base metals that are present in the package. After twenty minutes the crucible is removed from the furnace. The bead of pure gold and silver is cooled, rolled into a strip and then into a cornet shape. It is placed in a platinum thimble and put into boiling dilute nitric acid for fifteen minutes when it is removed, washed and the process repeated with stronger nitric acid. It is then removed, annealed and weighed. This treatment is known as 'parting', the silver being 'parted' from the gold by the acid. From its weight the gold content of the sample is calculated in parts per thousand. The accuracy is checked by testing a pure gold sample alongside the submitted sample. The assay office tests samples in batches of ninety-six at one time.

A weighed silver sample is tested by a procedure known as the 'Guy Lussac' method. The sample is put in a glass bottle, dilute nitric acid is added and the whole is heated until the sample is dissolved in the liquid. An exact amount of sodium chloride solution is added by means of a graduated pipette (a Stas pipette). The solution is of such a strength that all the silver in a normal solution sample would be precipitated as a silver chloride, leaving only one or two parts per thousand in solution. From the density of this cloud an experienced assayer is able to estimate the silver content of the sample. The tests are usually carried out with a proof sample in batches of thirty.

The method used for the assay of platinum is called atomic absorption spectrophotometry. It is far more involved than the methods used for testing silver and gold, and the most concise explanation is that supplied by the London Assay Office: 'In this method the sample is dissolved in aqua regia and the solution is sprayed into a flame through which is passed light of a selected wavelength emitted from a special lamp incorporating a platinum cathode. The amount of light absorbed is a measure of the concentration of platinum in the solution.'

Working properties of precious metals

Pure silver, known as fine silver, is very soft and therefore not directly made into silverware. It would dent easily and not be strong enough to withstand any wear, and so it is alloyed with another material. The same applies to gold. Many different alloys of silver, gold and platinum are produced by Johnson Matthey Metals, bullion dealers, and examples of the more common ones used are given below. These metals are produced by other bullion dealers, often under different names, so care must be taken to ensure that the right alloy is ordered. Solders are available to match all alloys listed and are dealt with in detail in Chapter 7. The working properties of silver, gold and platinum vary, and where these differences occur alternative methods of working are given.

Silver

Soft, white metal, second only to gold in malleability and ductility, which takes a highly reflective polish. When worked, silver becomes work-hardened and so must be annealed, or it will crack (the working properties vary slightly depending on the alloy being used). The melting point of pure (fine) silver is 962° C, specific gravity 10.50.

Standard silver 92.5 per cent silver, 7.5 per cent copper, is general, all-purpose silver, its assay mark is the lion passant.

Britannia silver 95.84 per cent silver, 4.16 per cent copper. Softer than standard silver, it is often used for enamelling as it contains a higher proportion of silver and less copper, which gives off an oxide. It is hallmarked with a Britannia stamp. It was first introduced in 1697 as a compulsory standard to replace sterling silver to prevent silversmiths of the time clipping or melting down coins of the realm to obtain their raw material, which was in short supply. Sterling was restored in 1720, but Britannia continued as an alternative.

Spinning alloy The original one contains cadmium and, as it is stronger and more malleable than the standard silver alloy, it is better for complicated spinnings. Standard silver hallmark.

Johnson Matthey spinning silver The same as the above alloy but it has no cadmium, so any scrap can be melted for casting without fear of dangerous fumes being given off. Contains zinc. Patent held by Johnson Matthey. It has a standard silver hallmark.

Hardenable silver This alloy contains approximately 83 per cent silver, 0.2 per cent magnesium, 0.15 per cent nickel. Its greatest asset is that it can be hardened by being put into a kiln, with a flow of air; this can be a standard enamelling kiln or burn-out furnace. The metal can also be bought prehardened. The amount of time the process takes depends upon the thickness or gauge of the metal: a thin sheet can take one hour, a thicker sheet takes longer.

37 Musical box in fine silver, raised,
decorated with mother of pearl. Diana
Hobson, 1977

No harm can come of prolonged heating, and the treatment temperature is not critical as long as the time is
sufficient to harden completely through the thickest
section, and the melting point is not reached (over
900° C). The hardening temperature should be between
650° C and 800° C, for each mm of section and both faces
of the sheet must be exposed to the atmosphere in the
kiln. Once hardened the process cannot be reversed.

The metal is soft and malleable, but it cannot be
annealed. It may be heated for 'stress relief' to between
300° C and 350° C, the temperature at which soap,
smeared on the surface of the metal, will char.

Because it is virtually pure silver the metal can be
raised, spun, forged, etc. and worked a great deal without
cracking. The prehardened alloy can be hot-forged,
although care must be taken to avoid cracking. The
softened alloy may be forged cold, but not hot-forged as
this will lead to surface hardening. The alloy cannot be
used for casting.

Another advantage of hardenable silver is that as there
is no copper in the metal, no firestain occurs (see p. 82).

The alloy is worked in its soft state, and hardening is not done until all but the simplest forming operations have been completed. Soldering is not carried out until *after* hardening. The prehardened alloy can be used for springs in boxes, money clips and other jobs where little forming is to be done, and a hard springy metal is needed. Both forms of the alloy come in wire, rod and sheet form. When buying the metal one should check to see if it has been hard-rolled. If this is so, it should be 'stress-annealed' very carefully by just burning soap on its surface. Scrap should be kept separate from other types of silver. Britannia hallmark.

Casting alloy   Standard silver casting grain which contains a scavenging agent that helps to deoxidize the alloy, producing better castings.

Chain-making alloy   Two different sorts of silver wire are produced for chain-making. One has a solder core running through it to help with the tricky problem of the soldering chain, which can be made up and passed through a furnace to be soldered. The other contains a percentage of cadmium which helps the soldering process. This is called the 'C' alloy and has a standard silver hallmark.

Enamelling grade   Standard silver with no impurities that can affect the enamel by changing the colour or by causing it to chip off.

Gold

This is the most malleable and ductile of metals. It anneals at a high temperature and care must be taken not to over-heat the metal, thus making it unworkable. Like silver it takes a high polish, hardens when being worked and so needs to be annealed. It is highly resistant to corrosion. The working properties vary slightly according to the alloy. The melting point of pure gold is $1063°C$, its specific gravity 19.32. Many of the alloys below are named after the firms which originally ordered them to be made up; others take the name obviously suited to them.

9 carat alloys
9 carat DF. General all purpose gold. Brassy-yellow colour.

9 carat P. Pin alloy. It is much harder than 9 carat DF, commonly used for pins on brooches and snaps. It is very springy.

9 carat CY. Casting alloy, yellow. De-oxidizing agent to help with casting.

9 carat green.

9 carat medium red.

9 carat s.c. A chain-making gold wire. Solid or solder core. Yellow.

9 carat deep drawing. Good for stampings. Ductile and strong.

9 carat white gold alloys

Hard white gold.

Casting white gold.

BW. General purpose, commonly used gold.

Soft white. Extremely soft, used most often for medallions and coins.

9 carat yellow, red, white and pale yellow enamelling alloys.

14 carat alloys

14 HB. General purpose yellow gold.

14 JP. Popular in Europe.

14 HY. Popular in the USA.

14 DR. Red alloy.

14 MW. Medium white alloy.

18 carat alloys

18 HB. An all purpose rich yellow gold.

18 HAB. Harder more springy version of HB.

18 CY. Casting alloy, yellow. Contains small amount of zinc to help the flow of the metal for sounder castings.

18 carat green.

18 carat AK and MR. Both red golds. MR (medium red) is darker than AK.

18 carat white

18 FW. Hard springy white gold.

18 MW. Medium white, all purpose. Generally thought a good colour.

18 WC. ⎫
18 BC. ⎬ Casting alloys. BC slightly softer.

18 SW. Very soft alloy. Used for coins and medallions.

22 carat

DS. Rich yellow.

22 R. Red.

Platinum

A grey, malleable metal that can be cast, forged and soldered, whose hardness makes it widely used in the jewellery industry. It work-hardens quickly and so has to be annealed more often than silver. When being worked it may attract on to its surface a layer of the metal of which the hammer or tool is made. To ensure purity when working platinum, it should be pickled in hot hydrochloric acid after it has been worked and before being annealed. It is not used often by silversmiths (although it was given a standard assay mark, an orb, in 1975), because of a) its price, b) its hardness which makes it difficult to spin and almost impossible to raise (though this problem can be overcome by careful annealing) and c) its reflective, but dull, grey finish. It is highly resistant to corrosion. The melting point of pure platinum is 1773.5°C, specific gravity 21.45.

GW. All purpose platinum.

HM. Harder alloy than GW.

ST. Spring alloy, used for pins and snaps.

CP. Soft casting alloy.

CO. Hard casting alloy.

SS. Extremely soft alloy.

Most of the metals in the above list are sold in a variety of forms, such as sheet, usually between G6 (0.40 mm) and G20 (1.65 mm), wire (square, round and rectangular), and tubing (thin-wall and thick-wall).

38 Raised silver bowl. Frances Loyen, 1971

6   Largework – raising and hammering

Largework is the general term covering hollow-ware (jugs, tea-pots, trophies, etc.) and flat-ware (trays, plates and other dishes). For these the techniques of raising and hammering are basic, and learning the correct way to use a hammer, carefully and in a disciplined manner, is one of the most important requirements of silversmithing.

Raising is the way to produce a hollow form of some depth from a flat sheet of metal without any soldering. To begin raising a piece, it is necessary to start with a drawing of a plan and side elevation or, if the piece is complicated, a full working drawing. The piece of metal, which should be circular, is called a 'blank'. The size of the blank is calculated by adding the average diameter to the full height of the job; to this must be added 'experience' since everyone has an individual way of raising; some stretch the metal, others compress it.

The thickness of the metal is determined partly by the type of metal used and partly by the design. The most common size is G12 (0.90 mm). If Britannia silver or copper is used, either is more likely to thicken up, and G11 (0.80 mm) would be more suitable. When raising is first being practised, gilding-metal is better to use than copper as its working properties are nearer to those of silver. After the formula for the size of the metal has been worked out, take a pair of dividers and scribe the correct size of the circle on to the metal. Cut out this piece with metal shears.

Annealing

When a piece of metal has become work-hardened through being hammered and needs to be softened so that it will not crack, it will feel hard and springy. Then annealing is required. Metal should be softened after every round of raising. The metal is heated to a temperature below its melting point and then quenched or allowed to cool slowly if certain gold alloys are being worked. The temperature at which the metal is annealed is important, as over-heating leads either to the metal

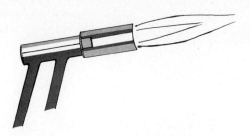

39 Flame for annealing

cracking or taking on an orange-peel-like surface, show-ing that the grain structure has been enlarged to such an extent as to make the metal unworkable. Over-heating will also cause heavy oxidization on silver and gold if the heating is done in air, producing firestain (see p. 82). The recommended temperature at which precious metals should be annealed is approximately 650° C, producing a dull red colour. At 700° C the metal will glow a good red, at 500° C the red glow will go out of it. If the temperature is not high enough, the metal will not be fully annealed. Care should be taken with platinum. It will work-harden faster than the other precious metals, but should not be over-annealed as this leads to a 'heat-etch' pattern developing on its surface. Anti-firestain solution is not needed on platinum, as there is no danger of an oxide film forming on its surface.

There are several ways of heating the metal: different gas torches are available for use with cylinders or com-pressor and natural gas (see p. 78). The flame is shaped rather like two cones, one inside the other, just beyond the tip of the inner cone. Regardless of the type of appliance used, the hottest part of the flame is always at the same point.

When any metal is to be heated, always make sure that the hearth is clean so that nothing can be burnt on to the surface of the metal, from which any unknown marks should immediately be scraped or filed off.

While it is still dark red, the metal should be quenched in cold water. As a general rule quenching makes a great difference in the softening process of the metal, but there are exceptions: Johnson Matthey state in their catalogue that certain of their golds should not be quenched; others may be quenched once the metal has cooled to black heat (450° C–500° C) and others must be quenched from above 500° C. (See also p. 106.)

The piece of metal should then be dropped in the pickle (see p. 19) which cleans off any dirt and oxide. Silver and gold only need to be pickled after they have been annealed for the first time, or if they have picked up dirt on their surfaces. With gilding-metal the piece should be pickled every time it has been annealed as a thick copper oxide forming on its surface. If this is not removed it gets hammered into the surface which then becomes pitted and discoloured. After the initial pickling, a layer of fine silver or gold is left on the surface of the metal, and remains there until it is broken either by polishing or filing. This fine silver gives a soft white sheen to the metal, and fine gold a buttery yellow sheen. Gilding-metal and copper are very dirty to work with, even after they have been pickled.

Blocking

This is the first stage of hammering a flat sheet into a dish shape in order to provide a firm form on which to work. (It is easier to hold than a flat sheet of metal which would buckle when hammered on to a metal former.) The blocking hammer, one of the heaviest hammers, is used. It can have a face ranging from full to large and domed, and measure up to 5 cm.

If the job is to have a flat base, a circle with the diameter equal to that of the base should be marked from the centre of the blank, using pencil compasses rather than dividers as the cut made by dividers could easily open when the metal is hammered. If the piece is to have a curved bottom, the circle should be marked at the appropriate point where the metal begins to curve round on the drawing, and it should be raised in the same way as a flat-bottomed piece, the bottom being blocked out into a sandbag after the job has been raised completely. The

40 Blocking

reason for keeping the centre circle true is that, having a centre point, everything can be measured from it. (See below, *Back-raising*.)

The blocking is done in recesses cut in a firm wooden block, a steady, traditionally a tree-trunk. Wood gives easily under the metal, neither stretching nor marking it. A hollow about 12 cm across and 4 cm deep is scooped out of the surface of the wood and the metal is blocked into it with the hammer.

A series of concentric circles, to be used as guide-lines, should be drawn from the base circle to the outside edge, using a pencil compass. Draw in a pencil line from the centre of the blank to the outside edge and, starting from this line, taking the outside circle first, the metal should be hammered down on to the wood. After each hammer blow the metal should be revolved, until a full circle has been covered, back to the original pencil line. Care should be taken to ensure that the blocking hammer does not go over into the edge of the next inner circle. It is important that the base circle is facing *down* into the wood, as this part will become the outside of the job, its centre having been originally marked with dividers.

The blocking should be done slowly and methodically. The hammer is very heavy and should not be wielded energetically; correct hammering will produce a more precise, even shape. The job should only need to be blocked twice, that is, a full round of blocking from the outside edge, working round to the inside circle, anneal, round again, and anneal. It should now be a gentle curved shape with a flat base.

Raising

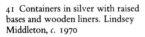
41 Containers in silver with raised bases and wooden liners. Lindsey Middleton, *c.* 1970

The metal is now ready to be raised. The centre (base) circle and concentric circles to the outside edge of the metal should be drawn in as before.

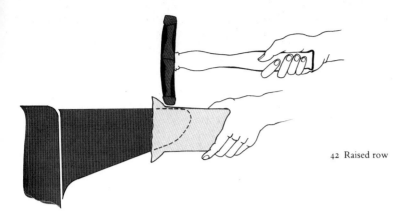

42 Raised row

The former used to shape the metal is a steel stake. Normally double-ended, this is sunk into a tree-trunk or clamped into a vice. A tree-trunk is better for the first stages of raising as it is necessary to sit down to use it. The position is more relaxed and the knee can act as a guide against which the metal can rest. It should not, however, act as a lever, as this would result in vibrations in the metal, causing uneven raising and bruised knees, apart from making the job very difficult to hold.

The type of stake, its size and shape, obviously depends on the shape of the job. For the early stages of raising, the profile of the stake should be convex, with the upper corner of the end rounded off, so that it does not cut into the metal. The bottom corner of the end of the stake should be dropped back at an angle to ensure better clearance for a form with inward sloping sides. If a proper stake is not available a round steel bar may be filed and modified, and used in a vice.

A raising hammer is used, its shape varying according to individual taste. Some people prefer a full hammer, others a narrow one. The basic requirement is that the face should have a curved, softened top edge, as a sharp edge would cut into the metal.

The metal is now put over the stake, the proposed starting point being in contact with the front corner of the stake. The metal is tipped up at an angle and the hammer-face dropped on to it, compressing it on to the stake. The handle of the hammer should be held high, so that the top edge of the hammer-face makes a distinct step on the surface of the job. The hammer must *compress* the metal. If the metal is struck on to the stake it will be stretched and thinned, and the raising will be uneven. The raised row should be obvious from the ridge it leaves around the work.

Each stroke should be next to the previous one and each row should overlap, otherwise the surface will have definite waves and bumps. The metal is hammered in rounds up to 5 mm from the top edge. The last round is

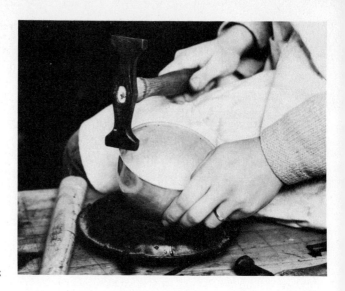

43 Caulking

done with a wooden mallet so that the edge does not stretch. A wooden mallet compresses the metal more than a hammer. If, during a raising, the metal is stretched too much, a complete course of raising with a mallet will compress it. Some people prefer to raise entirely with a mallet, which should have a sharpened, wedge-like face.

Caulking

The final stage of raising is the thickening of the top edge of a form, technically known as 'caulking'. It should be done at the end of every round of raising. The job is put on to a sandbag and hammered along the rim, which is thus thickened, but it may also cause the metal to turn over and crease so the job needs to be set against a stake and the edge hammered gently to flatten out any creases. This should all be done with a raising hammer. The sandbag is a circular-shaped heavy leather cushion, filled with sand, its diameter ranging from 15 cm to 20 cm. It absorbs hammer blows, thus preventing a piece of work from being damaged.

As the raising proceeds, the shape of the work should be checked with the original drawing, at first by eye, but in the later stages with a template. The job should be checked after each round to ensure that it is even. If one side is leaning, raise in only that side. If a flare develops, which happens when too much metal is taken in during the bottom rounds, start the raising high in the body until it is righted. With every stage in raising, make sure that the job is done as evenly as possible. If one stage is lopsided, the ensuing stages will also be lopsided.

Care must be taken not to over-heat the metal (see p. 60). This can happen as a result of inexperience, for, if the hearth is in a light part of the workshop, the correct colour of the heated metal cannot be seen. As experience is gained, the type of flame used and the appropriate length of time required will be easier to ascertain. Another way of telling whether or not a piece of metal has been annealed is to coat it with a flux that becomes fluid at a known temperature. If the piece develops small cracks, these can be soldered by hammering either side of the crack to close up the hole, cleaning the metal and soldering it with hard solder. The raising can then be continued, but with care as these parts are likely to split again if hammered too much. If the metal has been excessively over-heated, it will have to be scrapped entirely.

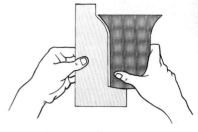

44 Template

The base of the piece should now be put on a base stake, the diameter of which should be slightly smaller than that of the job. It should then be malleted flat, and finally planished around its outside edge to harden and smooth it out completely.

Making a template

Make a tracing of the original drawing, warm it slightly and spread a thin layer of beeswax on to its surface. Leave it to cool. Rub the tracing gently face down on to the metal, and a clear replica of the drawing will be left. Cut this out carefully with a piercing saw.

Creasing

Creasing is a faster method of raising where a much thinner gauge of metal can be used, although it is better practised after some experience has been gained in ordinary raising. Before raising file a deep groove into a wooden block. Draw lines radiating from the centre of the metal, and with a collet hammer crease the metal into the wooden groove, increasing the pressure of each hammer stroke towards the top of the job. Anneal the metal and start raising in the normal way. Creasing may precede each raising as long as the block can be inserted into the work.

45 Creasing

Back-raising

This is a technique for thickening up the rounded bottom of an object, either because it is needed for extra weight or because the piece has been raised too high and needs to be reduced. It was originally used with tumbler cups where a rounded bottom provided sufficient weight to bring the vessel back to an upright position after it had been tilted over, even when its sides were horizontal.

A template is essential to make sure that the job remains even. A line should be drawn around the piece, and hammering should begin from there. The metal is

46 Back-raising

65

placed over a bottom stake and held up at an angle, exactly as in ordinary raising. The hammering is done in rounds, the only difference being that it finishes at one closed point rather than at an open top edge. The piece should now be planished.

Planishing and cross-planishing

Planishing is the smoothing of the metal by hammering its surface against a highly polished steel stake that fits the job perfectly, a technique that removes all lumps and any marks on the surface. The most important part of planishing is to find a stake to fit the job well, and it should not be too small as this can cause a ridge in the planishing; if it is too big, the shape of the piece will be altered. The correct size is a little smaller than the job to allow it some movement.

The method of raising a bowl shape with a curved base has been discussed on p. 61. Once the bowl has been raised evenly with a flat base, this base should be placed on a sandbag and the bottom knocked out with a pear-shaped mallet, a bossing mallet which has a domed face, or a bossing hammer.

If the base has been knocked out evenly, the final shape will need only to be planished for it to have an even finish. If, however, it has been stretched too far or is too uneven, it must be back-raised from a point just outside the original base line. The metal should be annealed, then scoured with pumice powder. The stakes and hammers should be cleaned and highly polished.

The planishing hammer has two faces, a square end and a round end. The square end, having a flatter face than the

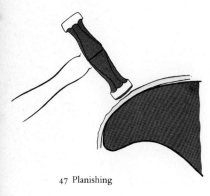

47 Planishing

48 Raised silver bowl. Michael Lloyd, c. 1970

49 Collet hammer

other, should be used on a piece that has straight sides, and the round end should be used on a more rounded, full shape such as a bowl. For a concave shape, a square-faced collet hammer that fits the curve of the piece should be used.

If the stakes available do not fit the job, one should be made or an old one should be filed to the correct shape. Several stakes can be used to planish one job, each fitting a different part, but care must be taken to ensure that the size of the stakes correspond where the piece is transferred from one stake to another. The stake used for planishing should be put in a vice, or in a 'horse' (see p. 24). The stake or head slots into the horse which is then clamped into a vice. As the arm of the horse is long and thin, the job can be more easily manipulated on the tool.

Planishing is best done standing up. The hammer should be in line with the tool and form an extension of the arm, used from the elbow. The piece should be placed on the stake and held lightly between thumb and forefinger. It should not be gripped tightly, but balanced, with the metal actually resting on the stake. Unlike raising, where the metal is compressed on to the stake, it is now pinched between the hammer and the stake, being stretched and smoothed out. The surface should be thoroughly cleaned as any dirt on the hammer or stake will immediately transfer a mark on to the metal.

The hammering should be rhythmic. Every hammer blow should overlap the previous one, as should every row of hammering. If done correctly, planishing should produce a ringing sound; if the metal is not resting properly on the stake, the sound will be hollow. The metal should be placed on the stake and the hammer pushed against the metal so that the point at which hammering should be started may be found. Before planishing is begun concentric circles should be drawn on the metal, about 1 cm apart, with pencil compasses (see p. 62).

If the raising hammer marks on the metal are difficult to remove the piece should be annealed and planished again. It should not be hammered on one spot too many times; if a mark is deep an area round the spot should be planished, otherwise a pimple of metal will be pushed up. Any ridges that have appeared should be cross-planished. When a long dish is to be planished, this should be done first clockwise, then anti-clockwise, to prevent the piece from twisting. It should also be cross-planished.

Cross-planishing should not be as close as straight-planishing, but should be done in a more open framework. Radial lines should be drawn from the centre of the piece, which should then be placed on the stake and hammered lightly but firmly, up and down across the ridges, following the lines. When planishing a curved base on a bowl the hammer work should be opened out towards the centre of the piece; if the centre is planished too heavily, a pimple will appear. If this happens, the piece should be annealed and the pimple knocked down. As one of the functions of planishing is to harden the metal, care should be taken *not* to raise a pimple, as the annealing necessary to remove it will soften the metal. A piece that has been planished too often will not only stretch beyond its original size, but will also become very thin.

Sinking a tray

This is a method of forming a piece from a flat sheet of metal that is to be shallow or of a medium depth. The method described below is for sinking a small circular tray; another method of sinking is by peening (see p. 126), used to produce a shallow bowl with a thick edge.

The tray to be sunk has a flat rim about 2.5 cm wide and a flat base, sunk about 2.5 cm. The flat sheet of metal should be cut out to the same size as the plan view of the tray, in this case, a 15 cm circle, and annealed. A circle is now drawn with a pencil compass inside the outer circle, indicating the desired width of the rim of the tray, that is a 12.5 cm circle, giving a 2.5 cm rim.

The stake to be used is a rectangular piece of hardwood, which is clamped in a vice, its top then being filed flat. An arc is now drawn (part of the circumference of the 12.5 cm circle) on to the flat top of the wooden block. It should not occupy too much of the surface of the wood, as enough space must be left to support the rim of the tray. The wood is now filed, forming a sharp edge along the line of the arc, with a half-round rasp, so that it drops almost vertically for 2.5 cm, and then tapers off. The top surface of the wooden stake will support the rim of the tray and allow the metal to be sunk without the hard filed edge of the arc cutting into it, which would happen if a metal stake were used.

The rim of the tray is now rested on top of the wood, and the part to be sunk struck with a dome-headed ham-

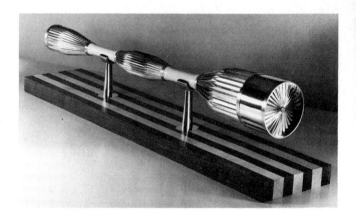

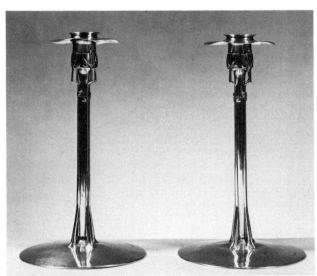

50 Raised silver mace with ivory. Gerald Benney. Cartier award, 1963

51 Pair of silver candlesticks. Rex Silver, 1906. Illustrates techniques of hammering, soldering and casting

52 Salt and pepper pots in raised silver with wooden bases. Lindsey Middleton, c. 1970

53 Raised silver goblets. William Phipps, 1970

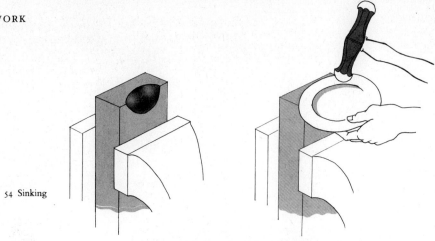

54 Sinking

mer. The metal is struck from the inside (12.5 cm) circle, moving inwards. The principle is to direct the blows of the hammer on the inner or concave surface of the metal, while resting what is to be the rim of the tray on a piece of wood. The metal is sunk on air, having nothing beneath to support it. As with raising, the hammering is done in rounds, starting at one point, and going round in a circle back to that point. The number of rounds depends on the design, on how deep the sinking should be, and on how much stretching of the metal is to be done in the particular case. The metal must be annealed between every round of hammering. After the first round of sinking, the metal will appear rather bumpy, but this is evened out with the next round. When the metal is sunk to the required depth, it should be planished, and only the part of the work that has been sunk should be worked on at this stage. It is held at an angle on to a flat steel plate, and planished with a planishing hammer, if it will fit into the space, or with a collet hammer.

As with straight-planishing, the metal is hammered between the steel hammer and the steel block, being smoothed, stretched and thinned, a technique that requires much practice. It is easy to sink the tray too far, and the only way to make it shallow again is to cut off the top, file it down and solder it together.

If the piece is to have a sharp edge where it joins the flat rim, it is put on to a flat metal stake and planished around the edges of the metal on both sides of the corner. Care should be taken to ensure that the sharp edge of the stake does not cut into the metal. Obviously the technique has to be adapted to the particular job. If the design does not have a sharp edge, it should not be planished on to a stake with a sharp edge, but on to one that has been rounded off.

To set the tray so that it is flat also requires much practice. It is important, as with all planishing, that the

metal is struck with the centre of the face of the hammer, rather than with its edge, in order to avoid denting and stretching the surface. When some experience of flattening metal has been acquired, a large setting hammer can be used. The tray should be annealed before the final planish. The previously hammered part of the job should be planished as explained above, leaving the outside rim and base until last. To complete these, the tray should be placed on a surface plate and hammered around the circumference of the base circle, on the inside of the job. This action will harden that part of the metal, which will pull the rest of the base flat. The same should be done with the outside edge of the rim; care should be taken not to catch the extreme edge of the metal with the hammer, thereby stretching it.

55 Planishing a sunk tray (incorrect way)

56 Planishing a sunk tray (correct way)

57 Church set in silver with sunk tray. Michael Lloyd, c. 1970

Seaming

This is a way of forming a piece, whether deep or shallow, by hammering or bending the shape from a single piece of metal into a cylindrical form, then soldering the edges together. Cylindrical forms are usually made by this method, which can also be used as a short cut to making pieces that would normally be raised. The form is made by malleting a flat sheet around a cylindrical steel stake. The flat piece of metal must first be filed true with each edge square to the next (see p. 95). It is annealed and malleted first from one end, then from the other, around the stake, being finally malleted completely round the stake until it is a cylinder. If the edges do not close, they can be pushed together by hand. The piece is then bound with binding wire around its circumference at several stages along its length and soldered with hard solder.

After pickling any excess solder is cleaned from the job, which is then malleted again around the stake. If the cylinder is bowed in the middle or splays out at the ends, which can be checked with a ruler held along its length, it may be straightened with a planishing hammer or even, if this is done firmly, by hand. If the centre is concave, it

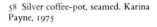

58 Silver coffee-pot, seamed. Karina Payne, 1975

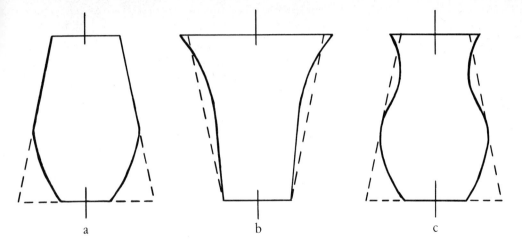

may be planished lightly to expand and lift it. If it bulges out in the centre, two small pieces of paper should be rested on the stake on each side of the bulge, which will lift the whole cylinder off the stake slightly. The bulge is then hammered lightly but firmly, and the metal will be pushed past the point required, but will spring back into the correct position. The edges may splay out, and to correct this the cylinder is slipped on to the stake, the offending edge overlapping the end of the stake. It is then hammered carefully on air into position. If the ends taper inwards, they can be planished to stretch them to the right size. All these corrections must be done carefully, every stage being checked with a ruler. A job will be ruined if it is stretched too much by over-hammering, and it is better to do as much work as possible by pressing and pulling with the fingers or by malleting.

59 Three different forms showing how a cone can be adapted

If the metal is thin, it can often be rubbed back and forth over the edge of the steel stake to smooth it out, but care must be taken not to stretch the metal too much or break through it. This cylinder can be made into a container, either by butting a base straight on to it or by mitring one into position (see p. 97).

A cone is also the basis of seaming, and is used when a coffee-pot, vase, or similar container is being made that would otherwise be formed by raising. When the size of the cone has been calculated (see Figs 59a, b, c), it must be developed to find the correct size blank (see p. 47), and then it can be raised in or stretched to achieve the intended shape.

Fig. 59a shows a form from which a cone can be directly extended. The top can be left, as it requires no stretching or compressing, and the base is raised in; a separate sheet of metal is soldered on for the base, to be butted or mitred in position.

Fig. 59b shows a form where the two widest points are taken to calculate the size of the cone. The neck and base are later raised right in.

60 Silver tea-pot and jug. Lindsey
Middleton, c. 1970

Fig. 59c shows a narrow form splaying out at the top. The cone is taken from an average size of the whole form. The narrowest point is the same, but the cone tapers out where the form stays narrow. The widest point of the form splays out but the cone at this point is slightly narrower. These calculations can be carried out on paper with a little practice, and with some thought as to how much metal is to be compressed and how much stretched.

The solder seam must always be done with hard solder. If it should split while it is being hammered, the edges of the crack must be pushed back together and soldered with hard solder. Hammering along this solder joint should be kept to a minimum.

Making handles and spouts

There are many variations but most of the shapes can be dealt with in a few examples, each of which can be adapted to suit a particular design. Handles and spouts can also be cast. (See Chapter 11 on *Casting*.)

An oval or round section handle　When designing a handle or spout it is a good idea to make up a model from plaster, wood or plasticine in order to work out the correct dimensions of the blank. (See Chapter 4 on *Technical Drawing*.) An oval or round handle, parallel or tapered, will need two straight or tapered strips of silver, one for the back and one for the front. The correct oval shape is filed into a steel bar, and the silver annealed and hammered into the groove with a collet hammer. The groove must cover a large section of the silver but need not be the same length, the silver being moved up as a section is hammered. The two sides are then fitted and soldered together (see p. 81). The sides should be filed free of solder and cleaned with emery cloth. One end of this oval or round tube is now plugged with a piece of wood and a mixture of rouge powder and water, or whiting and water, is poured into it, swilled round and poured out

61 Hand-raised silver jug with ebony handle. Probably Arthur Dixon, 1898–99

again, leaving a layer of the mixture on the surface of the metal. It is then stood in a bucket of sand and into it is poured molten lead, which has been melted first in a crucible kept especially for this metal. A piece of wood is turned to a cylinder with a dimension equal to that of the inside curve of the handle, and the oval or round tube malleted over it. Without the lead core the tube would collapse, and even with it there is a danger of the curve's wrinkling, so it must be bent very carefully. When it is curved to the right shape, it must be examined from every angle to see that the curve follows through properly and is not twisted. The lead is removed by hanging the handle over a pot and warming the metal with a gentle flame. To make sure that all the lead is removed, the article is dipped in hot hydrochloric acid and a cloth is run through it to wipe away all traces.

D-section handle This is made by taking two strips of metal for the back and front, the inner being shaped in a 'U' section, and the other a flat sheet bent to fit the curve of the inner sheet and then soldered on to it. The U section is made by taking a round steel bar and filing into it a groove of the right shape. The silver is then hammered into this with a collet hammer and curved to the

75

62 Raised silver and wooden coffee set.
Brian Fuller, 1979

shape of a handle. The metal will soon begin to lose its
contour, so a thin strip of gilding-metal should be soldered (with 'easy' solder, see p. 86) to the top and bottom
of the strip to hold it firmly in position while it is being
shaped. When the correct shape has been reached, it
should be planished on its outer surface and the gilding-
metal removed by boraxing the joint, heating it and
pulling the metal off when the solder begins to flow. The
end should be splayed out if necessary and any straightening up or twisting into shape is done at this point. The
other flat strip of precious metal is bent to fit the inner
handle and soldered into position.

Another way of making a handle is by means of a
box-like construction, which is scored, bent and soldered
into shape.

When a handle is to be fitted on to a tea-pot or a
coffee-pot, it is necessary to have insulators (silver con-
ducts heat much more quickly than any other material).
The handle is made as a whole and soldered on, a cut
being made with a sawblade a certain distance from the
body of the pot to mark the place where the insulators are
to be fitted. The sawcut also acts as an air hole, for, when a
hollow object is heated, the air expands and, if there is
nowhere for it to escape, apart from there being a potentially dangerous situation, the piece will explode, and be
ruined (see p. 91). When the handle has been soldered in
position, it is severed at the sawcuts.

It is more practical when designing the handle to make
sure that the splayed-out end, if there is to be one, has a
parallel passage in front of it to take the insulators. The
insulators must fit well and tightly over a wide area, long

enough to take a strong rivet without splitting; no amount of packing with filler is a substitute for this.

63 Raised silver and wooden tea set. Christian Dell, 1925

Non-metal handle   Handles can be made from materials other than metal, with less conductive properties, such as ivory, wood, nylon and resin. Ivory can be carved and filed easily. It takes a high polish after being rubbed with wet and dry paper, although it should never be polished with tripoli or rouge compounds as it stains easily. Toothpaste and whiting are both good for polishing, and can be used with water on a polishing mop. There are many different woods that can be employed, but they must be treated with a wax or a varnish to protect them and keep their surfaces clean. Cane is used in strips that are wrapped around a metal handle or in lengths that are steamed and bent to form the handle. Wood, ivory and cane are organic materials and react to changes in room temperature. Nylon can be cut, filed and polished and is extremely tough. It is available only in white, but can be stained certain colours. Resin can be cast from a model; it is strong and durable and takes a high polish, which, however, scratches badly with wear.

Spout   Usually designed with the handle, the shape being similar, it is made using the same basic methods. Where a spout bellies out at its base the metal is sunk slightly in wood, hammered into a lead shape or raised slightly; if it becomes thin while it is being shaped by sinking, it should be turned over and raised in. The lip of the spout may have to splay out, in which case a short tapered bit of steel is hammered into it.

7   Soldering

Soldering is the process of joining pieces of metal together by fusing a solder between them. Solder is an alloy of the parent metal with another metal of a lower melting point. Gold and silver are alloyed with zinc and copper to produce the appropriate solder. Several pieces of basic equipment are needed, according to the type of work being done. Whether smallwork or largework, it is useful to have a small torch and hearth for use at the bench and a large torch and hearth in a more enclosed part of the workshop.

Torches

There are several makes of torches on the market, some for natural gas to be used with an air-blower and others for bottled gas. If natural gas is laid on in the workshop a non-return valve is needed to prevent a blow-back of gas to the main supply. A natural gas torch will have two heavy duty rubber or plastic hoses running from it, one to take gas, the other air. The air-pipe is fitted to the air-blower which is operated by electricity, and when it is turned on a rush of air will be pushed out of the nozzle at the head of the torch. The gas supply is turned on at a tap and will escape from a nozzle, also in the head of the torch, enabling the two to mix when turned on. There are two levers or a knob at the point where the torch is held to cut off or control the flow of either the gas or air, so that the heat of the flame can be efficiently controlled. The gas is turned on first and lit, giving a soft, billowing flame that can be used for melting wax, pitch or drying metal. The air-lever is then turned and the more air pushed into the gas, the hotter the flame, but if too much air is pumped into the amount of gas being given off then the flame will be blown out.

The torch should be tried out with different test pieces in order to see the range of temperatures that can be achieved; wax, silver, pitch, steel can all be heated to see the different effects of the flame, which will help to make it easier to judge when soldering. The soft billowing yellow flame achieved from burning only gas will leave a deposit of carbon in the form of soot on the precious metal, which will hinder the process of soldering. When air or oxygen is added to the flame it becomes not only hotter, but cleaner; however, if too much is added it will form heavier oxides on the metal and only localize the heat, which will also hinder soldering. The best flame for soldering is called a reducing flame, where there is an excess of gas over oxygen.

Bottled gas (propane or butane) can also be used in the workshop and a number of different torches are made for it. A reduction valve is needed to prevent the gas from escaping too quickly, which would produce too large a flame to be manageable. Sievert and Flamemaster both produce a torch for bottled gas that has a variety of nozzles for different jobs. A range of torches that can be operated by natural gas or bottled gas with an air-blower that gives the same control of flame to bottled gas as it does to natural gas and air is produced by Adaptogas, who make a range of different size torches, the most commonly used for silverware being the T2 and T4 (the latter being the larger).

A different range of torches is available for bench-soldering. A French blowpipe runs on the same principle as the gas and air torch, but the air is supplied by blowing through a rubber hose. This is useful for very small pieces such as jump-rings and catches for boxes. The Adapto mouth-blown torch is better for smallwork, boxes, etc., producing a large flame that can also be turned down quite small. There is also a very small Adaptogas torch which runs on bottled gas and air. Oxy-acetylene can be used, and the flame turned down until it is soft; even so, it is still very hot and the metal can easily melt if the flame is not handled properly. Small portable torches are also obtainable. They have disposable butane or propane gas and propellant canisters, and are ideal for soldering small pieces that may need a small hot flame. A tool-supplier will often give a demonstration of different types of torches, and the industrial department of the British Gas Corporation can be very helpful.

Hearth

Whatever type of torch is used, the heat given off can be retained more efficiently if the hearth is well set up. A bed of charcoal embers can be used to solder articles placed in them if they are fanned and, with this principle in mind, the hearth should be set up to retain as much heat as possible. This large hearth is filled with pumice chips, which are bought in lump form and broken up. The work is rested or supported on these chips which reflect the heat back on to it. It is a good idea to have a steel framework supporting asbestos boards all around the

64 Small bench hearth filled with
pumice chips

hearth, making not only a dark area which is helpful for
soldering and annealing to allow the colour to be seen (see
p. 18), but also a means of keeping the heat in. When
soldering large vessels such as coffee-pots or trophies it is
necessary to build a wall of firebricks around the work to
retain the heat, otherwise the correct temperature for
soldering will not be reached or it will take so long to heat
that the work will sag, or the alloying metal will burn out
of the solder, making it unworkable. A charcoal block
made from either natural willow or compressed charcoal
can be kept in a small bench hearth with a wire grid for
soldering work that must be kept flat. A soldering wig is
rather like a flat bird's-nest made from iron binding-wire
on a metal stalk: the wire is twisted haphazardly and
fastened to a steel plate, allowing awkward soldering to
be pushed in amongst the wires and so held in position.

A small revolving hearth for the bench, filled with
pumice chips, can easily be made from a sheet of brass or
gilding-metal. A large one should be made from sheet
steel. A small bench hearth is made in brass because it is
normally made in the workshop. Brass is easier to work
than steel. A large hearth or tray can usually be bought
cheaply from a scrap yard and would be expensive to
make or buy in brass. For the small hearth take a sheet of
brass G12 (0.90 mm) 20 cm square and measure a 2.5 cm
border around the perimeter. Mark the line with a scriber
and cut out the 2.5 cm squares formed at each corner. The
brass is then annealed and the edges, up to the border line,
are malleted over a steel stake until all of the sides are
folded over and brought up at right angles to the bottom
of the sheet, thus forming the tray. Two pieces of brass
tubing, one fitting easily but not too loosely inside the
other, are now needed. The wider of the two should be
shorter than the other and is soldered with 'extra-easy'
solder (see p. 93) on to a small flat piece of brass sheet G12
slightly larger than its diameter. This part is now soldered, again with extra-easy solder, to the tray. the other
piece of tubing is soldered to a piece of plate, G20

65 Silver coffee-pot with ebony handle and knob. Raised in two parts and soldered. Joyce Boyd, 1975. Photo James Boyd

(1.65 mm) or thicker. The top will now revolve on the base. This small hearth is also filled with pumice chips.

Joining the parts

The pieces of silver to be joined must fit well; if they do not the joint will be insecure and look unsightly. No matter what grade of solder is used, there is always a difference in colour, so the fitting of the pieces must be exact, leaving the smallest possible gap for the solder to run through. A wider gap either makes this impossible or else it will be seen, and small pin-holes will appear on its surface, showing the porosity of the solder alloy. Silver-soldering relies on the capillary attraction between close-fitting sides, and joining an ill-fitting gap can only be achieved by blobbing a series of lumps on the surface of the joint, which is most unsatisfactory. When a joint is to be made from one sheet of metal such as a cylinder, the edges to be joined must be filed so that they fit. Then the action of pushing the two edges past each other and pulling them back allows them to spring together.

When silver is soldered it does not lie on the surface of the metal but alloys into the metal immediately surrounding it, though not if the metal has any grease or dirt on its surface, so cleanliness is highly important. Both edges of the metal and the surrounding surfaces to be joined must be cleaned well before being soldered, and this can be done in several ways, depending on the work to be soldered. They can be lightly filed, scraped or rubbed with emery paper, after which they must not be handled in order to keep the area free from grease. Any dirt on the surface, oxide, grease, rouge or even a pencil mark, can stop the solder from running. When a job entails bringing one piece of silver on to another, more preparation is necessary. The area around which a spout is to be soldered on to a tea-pot should be filed or scraped free of firestain and dirt, and polished to a good finish. It is then cleaned with washing-up liquid and water to remove any polishing compound left on the surface, and the point at which the spout is to be soldered is marked with a scriber. The area just inside this line is then scraped to roughen the surface slightly. The point of polishing the metal so well before soldering is to leave a surface that can be finally polished without corners and edges being polished off, giving a much better result.

Firestain

The formation of an oxide on or just under the surface of the precious metal causes a blemish which can be minimized by use of an anti-firestain solution. Borax or Argotect can be used or else the following solution can be made in the workshop: 600 ml industrial methylated spirits, 150 ml acetone, 60 ml boric acid crystals, and 15 gm borax powder. This is painted on the metal before it is heated. Low carat golds take on firestain more easily than the higher carat golds, which usually have to be over-heated before they will oxidize. Firestain can be prevented to a large extent by not over-heating the metal or putting it through the fire too many times.

The removal of firestain by dipping an article in hot nitric acid or rubbing with the abrasive water of Ayr stone is usually carried out in the finishing stages (see p. 172) or during individual solderings when it would prevent the solder from flowing. Dipping in nitric acid may cause the metal to take on a heavy texture. To stop this happening, the dipping must be done quickly and the piece then rinsed, any remaining firestain being taken out with the abrasive. Firestain can be seen if, after the metal has been pickled in sulphuric acid, it is held in front of a white card. Dark cloudy patches will show on the metal if firestain is present, which may cover the whole piece. If it is filed, the clean metal will show through. The firestained surface can only be broken by filing or by some other abrasive method such as polishing, not by hammering.

Methods of binding

However well the pieces fit together, they must be bound in some way to hold them in position. When the metal is heated it will expand, the action of the flux bubbling up

and the solder moving all tending to push the metal apart. Once the pieces have been bound or held together firmly in some way, one's attention can be given entirely to soldering the piece rather than trying to juggle it around and solder at the same time.

There are several methods of binding, depending on the piece of work. For a straight cylinder binding-wire, made of soft iron is used, which is available in several thicknesses. It should be doubled and twisted so as to retain its malleability and give extra strength. A tightening loop is then twisted half way along its length and the wire wrapped around the circumference of the piece. The ends are twisted together and, with the centre loop, have now become tightening loops which distribute the tension so that pressure is placed evenly against the sides that are to be joined. Depending on its length, a long cylinder will need several bands of binding-wire or the ends will escape the tension.

A seamed cone will need extra binding to stop the wire slipping up to one end. A length of wire is hooked tightly over each end of the cone, small loops being first twisted down its length every 1 cm. Shorter lengths are then wrapped around the cone passing through the loops which hold them in position and are tightened, as are those on a cylinder, by a twisted loop at one end and a twist in the wire at the other.

A vessel such as a bowl that is to have a foot-ring soldered to it should never be bound with wire stretching across its mouth, which is a sure way to distort it. A hook should be bent on to each end of the wire and latched on to the rim of the inverted bowl. Two loops are twisted at the two points where they touch the base ring to hold the wire firmly in position without danger of distorting the bowl.

66 Binding a base wire around its circumference

67 Binding a base on to a cylinder

68 Binding a cone

69 Cutting stitches

Methods of securing

Another way of holding a wire in place is to use 'stitches', which are often combined with binding-wire. After the job has been cleaned in preparation for soldering, a line is scribed on to the metal outlining the position of the piece to be brought on. So that the cuts do not show after soldering, a series of 'V' section cuts are made from inside this line with a graver going up to it. A graver is a small tool used by an engraver: the mushroom handle is held in the palm of the hand and the tool is pushed along through the metal. At the end of every stroke an engraver will flick the tool to remove the metal from it. To form a stitch a short line is cut but the metal is thrown up vertically and left, rather than being flicked away. To hold the piece in position a series of stitches is made following the scribed line. Once the job has been soldered the stitches are removed carefully with a needle file.

If a thin wire is to be soldered, it is often easier to hold it together with small steel clamps or cotter-pins rather than binding-wire, and these should always be annealed and allowed to cool (steel softens when cooled slowly, non-ferrous metals only are quenched) before use so as to form an oxide on the surface of the metal which will prevent it from being soldered to the job. A small cotter-pin is broken in half and one piece bent to fit the curve of the wire, and clamped at either side of the joint by two stronger cotter-pins or a strip of steel 2 mm thick bent double to form a small strong clamp. The wire is then soldered.

bent double to form a small strong clamp. The wire is then soldered.

For small or awkward jobs where binding is impossible, soldering clay or plaster of Paris can be used to hold the pieces in position. The former contains a lot of moisture which will burn out when heated, but it should be used sparingly in order to allow the piece to get hot. The parts are cleaned and stuck into the soldering clay. It is better to put the clay straight on to a firebrick rather than into a tin lid which helps to retain the moisture. As soon as the clay is heated it begins to dry out and, if it is in a container, the steam cannot escape. To use plaster of Paris the parts are set up in wax. Plasticine should not be used as it is more difficult to remove from the metal and can cause an oxide on its surface. Plaster is poured on top of the job and when it is set the wax is pulled off. The parts to be joined are scraped clean of wax and plaster, boraxed and soldered. The plaster should only be used in small quantities but enough to complete the casting in one mix.

Asbestos paper can be used like soldering clay, it is mixed with water to form a claylike substance, pushed into position and then dried with a blowtorch. All these methods can be used, not only for holding the parts in position, but also to protect any thin wire or sheet that is likely to be melted during the soldering. A clamp called a 'third arm' can be purchased to hold wires in position while they are being soldered. Spring tweezers are also useful for the same purpose.

Fluxes

After the vessel has been bound together it must be protected by a flux. Its purpose is to keep the surfaces that are to be soldered free from dirt and oxides that may form during this process. There are several different fluxes on the market; the one most commonly used is borax, a crystalline salt which, when heated, bubbles up in a white porous mass and then settles down, fusing into a film of glass. It is bought in the form of a borax cone which is ground to a creamy paste in a small tray and then applied with a brush. Borax also comes in powder form, but this tends to go hard and lumpy. Liquid fluxes such as Auflux have the advantage of not bubbling up when first heated, but unless they are applied carefully tend to run over the parts of the work that are not to be soldered, risking the solder also running that way. Easy-flo flux, a white powder that is mixed with water to a paste, is a low melting-point flux normally used with easy and extra-easy solders. Johnson Matthey also specify it in their catalogue for certain gold solders. It can be used to help hard-solder joins that are not running easily by cleaning them, although it will burn out at a high temperature. Johnson Matthey also produce a high temperature one called Tenacity Flux No. 5. If, when the flux is applied, it separates and forms pools on the surface of the metal, it means that the surface is greasy and cannot have been cleaned properly. The flux must then be washed off with water, the metal cleaned and the flux reapplied.

Silver-soldering

When the flux has been successfully applied the vessel is ready for soldering. A thin wire grid or cotter-pins are placed on the revolving hearth containing firebricks or pumice chips. The metal has to be brought up to an even temperature all over for the soldering to work. If the metal is placed straight on to a cold solid surface such as a firebrick, most of the heat is taken away from the metal and the required temperature is not reached; hence the need for the grid or pins on which to place the metal. Often, if the piece of work is large or made up of struts, a wall of firebricks is placed around it to retain and equalize the heat. The wire grid or cotter-pins raise the piece of work from the stand, ensuring that it is heated from all sides, creating an even temperature. The work must always be supported properly or it will warp or sag; wires sticking out are likely to droop, and flat sheet, such as in a straight-sided box, can easily twist. Flat sheet can be strengthened by putting the U-section steel struts from an umbrella along the edge of the metal.

The type of soldering done by silversmiths is called hard-soldering, for which a silver (or gold) alloy of hall-markable quality is used, that is available in several grades, 'hard' and 'easy' being used most often. Easy solder should not be confused with soft solder used by plumbers, which is lead-based.

Silver-soldering may be done by using a stick of solder or paillons (small snippets of solder). The former is generally used by largeworkers, the latter by smallwork-ers. The problems that arise with soldering in these two categories of silversmithing are different, but the basic principles are the same.

Stick-soldering

The stick is filed clean, charged with flux and fed into the joint, being held in pliers or spring tweezers. The vessel is then heated. The flame used is hotter than that used for annealing metal, but it is not a hot concentrated one. It should be bushy, the metal being heated from just beyond the tip of the blue inner cone. The hearth is slowly turned with the right hand. It may feel clumsy at first for a right-handed person to hold the torch in the left hand, but with practice the torch can be operated with one hand, leaving the other free to turn the hearth and apply the solder. The flame should be kept moving,

heating the whole piece up to temperature. As the metal turns a bright red the flame is altered to a smaller, hotter more concentrated flame by turning the gas down, thus increasing the air, and then is run along the joint. The stick of solder must then be held in the flame for a moment to warm it slightly and applied to the joint. If the metal is 'to temperature', the solder will feed in immediately. As soon as the flash of solder is seen along the joint the flame must be removed. If the joint is long then the flame must be pulled along the length of it, and the solder will be drawn towards it. It is often easier with a long joint to pull the solder along half way and then apply it from the other end of the line, joining up the two in the centre. If a line of solder is heated for too long the zinc in it will burn out, resulting in pin-holes. When the joint has been soldered the piece of work is kept up to heat, turned over and heated on the other side of the joint. The solder will pull through the joint towards the flame, ensuring a sound result. The danger with stick-soldering is that too much can be applied which may be hard to remove and, if it is in too awkward a position, it may be impossible to remove. There is also a danger of over-heating and burning the solder into the surface of the metal when soldering the corners of boxes.

If too much solder has been applied the work should be heated to temperature and tipped up at an angle to allow the solder to run downwards: for this process a piece of copper or gilding-metal is placed at the bottom of the vessel touching the solder line and heated to a higher

70 Silver dish with individually soldered wires decorated with amethysts. Robert Welch, *c.* 1960

87

temperature than the vessel; as the solder runs, it is guided by the flame down on to the base metal and, if the metal is hot enough, the solder will pull down on to it. This method should only be used as a last resort as there is a danger of the precious metal being over-heated or melted.

Soldering a napkin-ring

A strip of metal is cut and filed to the correct size (found by multiplying the required diameter of the ring by π, or $3\frac{1}{7}$ or 3.14). It is filed true with the aid of a ruler and engineer's square (see pp. 95 and 96) and malleted over a parallel steel stake to form a cylinder. The two edges to be joined are sprung together (see p. 80), cleaned and boraxed. To get a good joint the edges are pushed together and cut through along the existing gap with a fine sawblade, but practice is necessary before a straight line can be achieved. Wire now binds the cylinder and is looped at the joint, the free ends being tied together diametrically opposite.

A stick of hard solder is then boraxed and held in tweezers, the ring placed on the hearth, either amongst the pumice chips or on a wire grid on a firebrick, the joint standing vertical to the hearth. The flame is concentrated on the ring, the point just beyond the inner blue cone playing over the whole job. The hearth is spun slowly with the right hand and, as the metal comes up to temperature, the gas lever is turned down giving a harsher blue flame. The solder is held in the right hand, warmed slightly and, as the gas is turned down, it is fed into the joint. The solder will feed in quickly and, as the flash of silver is seen along the joint, the torch is pulled along it, drawing the solder with it. The ring is then turned over and brought up to temperature, drawing the solder through to the inside. The piece is quenched and pickled.

If the napkin-ring is to have decorative wires around the edges, these are made by taking lengths of wire equal to the circumference of the ring and malleting them round on a stake. The circumference of this stake should be just slightly smaller than that of the ring. The lengths are then clamped together with cotter-pins and soldered with hard solder. After being quenched and pickled, any excess solder is removed and the wire rings are again malleted round on a stake. The napkin-ring is also malleted round and both edges are cleaned with emery paper to remove any dirt and firestain. The first of the smaller rings is placed flat on a wire grid and heated to cherry red. It will expand and the cool napkin-ring can be pushed quickly into it, when the narrow ring will immediately contract around it. The same process is applied to the other rim; when both are in position they can be boraxed and soldered, using easy solder, because

there are now three hard solder joints which would be likely to open if heated again to the temperature of hard solder. The napkin-ring is pickled, any excess solder filed off and the piece is ready for polishing.

71 Silver napkin-rings with textured decoration. Christopher Lawrence, c. 1970

Paillon-soldering

The paillons are cut from sheet. After the sheet has been filed small parallel cuts 1 mm apart are made in the sheet-solder with jeweller's shears. These are cut across 1 mm apart to form small squares of solder, then dipped in flux and applied to the job before heating.

If the joint is to be paillon-soldered, the snippets of solder are applied before the metal is heated. Heating should be done slowly as the flux will bubble up and the paillons jump off or out of position, they must be pushed back with tweezers. The flux should now settle down and the heating is carried on as for stick-soldering. When the metal is brought up to temperature, the paillons will flush along the joint: if there are not enough paillons more can be applied, but it is better to try to calculate the amount of solder needed before starting as constant heating and reheating will weaken the solder and distort the silver. The disadvantage of paillon-soldering is that if the metal is slightly over-heated, marks will be burnt into the surface where the solder has been and may be difficult to remove. As with stick-soldering, the piece of work is turned over and the solder pulled through the joint.

89

Charging with solder

If two sheets of metal are to be soldered flat together they should first be charged with solder to ensure a complete join all the way through, by cleaning the two faces and cutting small grooves with a file on the surface of each. The grooves are flushed with paillons of solder. The pieces of metal are then clamped together and heated again until the solder can be seen running along the edges of the metals. If the two sheets are to be drilled through, then grooves are not cut in the metal: instead the paillon of solder is sandwiched between the two pieces of metal and the whole piece clamped together. When the metal is heated the solder will fuse into both sides of the precious metal which will unite. When fitting a decorative wire along the edge of a piece of sheet, a groove is filed with a three-square needle file into the thickness of the metal and flushed with solder; the wire is put in place and the whole piece soldered. The result is a very neat joint, as the solder will not show.

Problems in soldering

Soldering should be done as quickly as possible. Constant reheating of the metal will make it sag and may over-heat the solder, causing its melting point to go up, the zinc in the alloy having been burnt out. Pin-holes will appear in the surface of the solder and it will not run. It must then be cleaned from the metal and the whole piece resoldered. A joint that will not run properly can be encouraged with an application of Easy-flo flux, but if the solder will still not run the piece must again be cleaned and resoldered. If the metal is not brought to temperature all over, the solder will form blobs and refuse to run. All excess solder must be removed from the joint after every soldering.

Soldering together two pieces of metal of different sizes and weight can prove difficult. If the flame is played equally on both pieces of metal the lighter will take the heat faster and may melt: if solder has been applied, it will immediately stick to the hotter piece of metal. If there is a great difference in the size of the pieces then the heavier part must be brought up to temperature first, the flame being played on that part only. The heat from this will pass through to the lighter piece of metal, which may not have to be heated with the flame. The solder will then run equally between the two.

If a part of a vessel does melt it can often be repaired by cutting out the damaged area, cleaning off any solder and then soldering a well-fitting piece of sheet into place. Pin-holes can be repaired by drilling them out and plugging them with silver wire the size of the hole. Trying to fill the pin-holes with fresh solder does not work; new ones will appear. If a piece has been soldered in the wrong position it can be boraxed, heated all over and quickly removed with tweezers. Any joints near by should be boraxed as well or painted with rouge powder and water to protect them. If they are boraxed, the solder is likely to reflush and the joint will move; if painted with rouge, care must be taken not to over-heat the joint or it will become brittle. If nothing is painted over the surrounding joints, then the solder on them can burn off. When several joints near to each other are to be soldered the same procedure applies, unless they can all be soldered at the same time.

If a silver wire, such as that used to thicken the top edge of a bowl, is wrongly positioned and has to be removed, a line should be scribed along the solder line to break the surface of the solder. The wire should also be cut at intervals into sections as it will be impossible to lift the whole wire off in one go. After boraxing the piece is heated to temperature and the sections of wire pulled out with pliers. If the metal is heated too much the wire will crumble and the flame must be removed in case the whole vessel is over-heated. This operation will probably require two people.

When designing silverware the placing of solder joints should be carefully thought out. They must be strong but unobtrusive. The different weights of pieces to be joined should also be considered. Too heavy a footing on the base of a bowl will cause a line to show on the inside of the bowl, especially if the job has been slightly over-heated or heated too slowly when being soldered. A straight stem that is soldered on to the 'cup' of a goblet will often show on the inside of the goblet unless it has been soldered extremely carefully or designed with a splayed-out end at the point where it is to be soldered. If a narrow wire has to fit on a vessel end on, it is better to solder this wire on to a small piece of sheet before soldering it into place. This dissipates the load and will stop the wire from wrenching the side of the vessel; it will also avoid a sunken mark on the inside.

When completely enclosed hollow pieces are being soldered, an air hole must be drilled at some point before the final piece of metal is soldered into position to avoid an explosion. The hole is drilled at a point where it is not too conspicuous, but it must allow the air to escape easily. When the piece has been soldered, allowed to cool and pickled, it must be boiled in household soda to neutralize the sulphuric acid. It should then be shaken and very gently heated in order to evaporate the liquid inside, taking care to avoid the steam which comes out of the air hole very quickly. Once the hollow is dry, and the metal is not going to be heated again, the hole can be plugged with a piece of tight-fitting tapered-round wire.

There are some differences between soldering gold and silver. When gold is brought up to temperature, which happens very quickly, it is more difficult to see its colour and thus it is easy to melt accidentally, so it has to be carefully watched. The edges of the sheet or wire will glow first, an indication that the metal is nearly to soldering heat. Platinum needs a white heat to reach the correct soldering temperature and it is often easiest to surround the piece with charcoal before heating it.

The type of solder to be used when constructing silverware depends on the number and positioning of the joints. Most will be done in hard solder, the last one usually in easy solder. If there are many joints, as happens in smallwork, however, then medium solder should be used.

The following list of solders is based on information supplied by Johnson Matthey.

SILVER

Solder	Melting point	Uses
Enamelling (Flux: borax or Tenacity No. 5.)	730–800° C	Used for work that is to be enamelled, although hard solder is just as good for doing this job. When being used it is likely to stay tacky unless heated carefully. The precious metal must be heated up to temperature and the solder applied to the hot metal without the flame coming into contact with the solder. It is, therefore, better used in stick form. Paillons can be applied once the job has reached soldering temperature. The melting point is very near that of silver.
Hard (Flux: borax or Tenacity No. 5. Easy-flo on some occasions.)	745–78° C	A solder most commonly used. The colour closely resembles that of standard silver. Strong ductile joints.
Medium (Flux: borax or Tenacity No. 5.)	720–65° C	Used chiefly in smallwork (and jewellery) where there are likely to be more joints in close proximity. An extra grade of solder means that the temperature of the metal does not have to be brought up to the heat of the first solder used thus helping to eliminate the risk of melting the first joints.

Solder	Melting point	Uses
Easy (Flux: borax or Easy-flo.)	705–23°C	More yellow in colour than hard solder. Used in largework as the next grade down from hard solder, but only if several hard-solder joints have been made, and another would be likely to damage them.
Extra easy (Flux: Easy-flo.)	667–709°C	Very yellow. Often used for silver repairs.

GOLD

There are gold solders to match the different gold alloys on the market.

Yellow	Flux	Melting point
9 carat extra easy	Easy-flo	640–52°C
9 carat easy	Easy-flo, borax	650–720°C
9 carat medium	Easy-flo, borax	735–53°C
9 carat hard	Tenacity No. 5, borax	756–93°C
14 carat easy	Easy-flo, borax	661–760°C
14 carat hard	Tenacity No. 5, borax	750–86°C
18 carat easy	Easy-flo, borax	630–710°C
18 carat medium	Easy-flo, borax	732–65°C
18 carat hard	Tenacity No. 5, borax	738–838°C
EGY 800	Tenacity No. 5, borax	866–77°C

Red		
9 carat red	Tenacity No. 5, borax	734–84°C
18 carat red	Tenacity No. 5, borax	796–819°C

White		
9 carat white	Easy-flo, borax	710–43°C
EWG 500	Easy-flo, borax	690–711°C
MWG 588	Easy-flo, borax	703–20°C
HWG 833	Tenacity No. 5, borax	853–85°C

72 Silver container. Michael Rowe, 1978

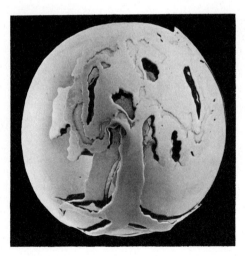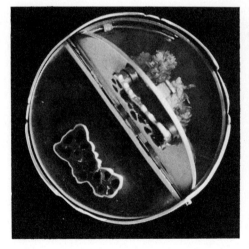

73, 74. *Left*: Silver box decorated with a pierced silver tree. Frances Loyen, 1975. Photo Laural Wade. *Right*: Silver and enamel box. Frances Loyen, 1975

8   Smallwork – fitting

Smallwork is the general term used to describe different types of box-making and other work that entails more fitting than hammering, such as watch-cases, powder compacts and picture frames.

Filing

In order to be able to fit metals together well, one must learn the proper technique of filing, which is not just a way of cutting the metal; it has to be done true and flat. One basic rule to remember in smallwork is that every part, as far as possible, should be measured from another part that is known to be 'true'. If a square box is being made, every stage of it should be made accurately, with this in mind. To square up a piece of metal, it should be cut very slightly larger (but by no more than 1 mm) than is needed. One of the longer sides is filed first; a metal ruler is placed along the edge of the sheet which is held up to the light. If the edge is not flat, the light will shine through the low spots, and in order to straighten it the high spots must be filed down. Hold the metal firmly against the pin, the edge to be filed facing upwards; file it *along* its length, rather than across it, since the latter method rolls the edge and does not give a flat finish. The file is held by the handle and the movement should come from the shoulder rather than the wrist: the file should be treated as an extension of one's arm and the work held parallel below it. If the metal is firmly supported, it will need only a few strokes to straighten it. If it is not done correctly, it may eventually become flat, but will not have the necessary accuracy and crispness. Note that the cutting action of the file is in the forward stroke: neither the file nor the metal need be grasped tightly, just firmly, otherwise one's arm will begin to ache and the work will suffer. The burr which appears at the edges of the cut when the metal is being filed must be taken off with the file or a scraper, and care must be taken to remove only the burr, not the edges of the metal. After every few strokes the metal is held up to the light with the ruler and

75 Truing up a piece of sheet

checked until it is completely flat. If the file has been quite flat against the metal, all the high spots will have been filed off after several strokes. The other edges of the metal are filed square to this flat one (now referred to as side 1). An engineer's square should be used. This is a right angle made from steel with precise machined sides, the shorter and heavier one being called the stock, the other the blade. The stock is held firmly against side 1, the blade showing the correct angle to which the adjacent side (side 2) should be filed. Light will again be seen at the low spots, and the high spots will need to be filed off. Proceed as with side 1, and then with sides 3 and 4.

Another way to square up a piece of metal is to use a vernier gauge, a measuring instrument with two faces which can be moved apart and back together again, staying straight and parallel. The measurement of distance between the faces is shown on a slide rule attached to them. The gauge is used rather like an engineer's square, the metal being put against it and held up to the light, but in this case the metal is put between the two edges which show if the metal is straight and opposite edges parallel. It is useful when making several pieces of the same shape, since the measurements can be checked at the same time as they are being filed. Ideally a shape should be made true at as early a stage as possible; a piece of metal with round corners or bevelled edges should always be filed straight and the corners taken off afterwards. If a complicated shape is to be made, it can often be cut out as a square or rectangular piece of metal unless it is completely asymmetrical. A straight edge can be cut into with a round, half-round, square, or any other shaped needle file to produce the required shape.

Mitring

Joining pieces of metal together at a right angle or any other angle to be held together in some way, normally by soldering, may be carried out by cutting an appropriate angle into the edge of the metal. For a square box the angle cut is 45°, forming a right angle when the two sides are joined together. The mitre reduces the width of the solder line to a narrow streak that can hardly be seen and cuts out the possibility of pin-holes appearing in the solder join, which can happen if two pieces of metal are butted together. The edges of the metal are first filed true and the thickness of the metal to be mitred is measured with a pair of dividers. The measurement is transferred on to what will ultimately be the inside face of the metal from the top edge. The metal is then rested firmly against the pin and filed from the back edge of the metal to the scribed line (a 45° angle). Again the metal is held stable and in line with the file and the arm. It is important that the mitre is accurate so that the two sides fit properly. When both edges have been filed they can be soldered, and should fit with only a line showing along the edge where they meet.

Butt joint

The bottom of a box can also be joined to the body by butting. Simply make sure that the two pieces fit together well, and solder them in place. The disadvantage is that a thin yellow line will show where the pieces are joined and there is a chance that pin-holes will appear along the line. It is, however, a much quicker method than mitring and does not require so much work or patience with the fitting of the pieces. If a base is being soldered on to a cylindrical box, the cylinder is placed on the sheet of metal and a line is drawn at the junction of the two. Stitches are cut up to this line from the outside to hold the box in position when it is bound with wire and soldered. Without the stitches the cylinder would distort when heated and become trapped in the distorted shape when the solder runs. After the cylinder has been cleaned the excess metal is cut away and the piece is filed. It should always be filed around the box to ensure that the edge at the bottom of the box is in line with the sides of the cylinder.

Drilling

A bench, hand, or pendant drill may be used, though one can achieve most precision with the first. The chuck on the drill holds the drill-bit, and is tightened and released with a chuck key, which must always be removed before the motor is switched on. Drill-bits are available in many different sizes, their measurements being given in metric and imperial sizes. Once the correct size and place where the hole is to be drilled have been decided, a mark of pin-head size is punched into the metal with a centre-punch. An automatic one is the quickest and easiest to use, being pressed down sharply with one hand to make the mark, the depth of which can be adjusted. A manual centre-punch is held in one hand and struck with a hammer held in the other hand.

Once the mark is made, the bit is put into the chuck, and the hole is drilled. A small piece of wood is placed on the bed of the drill to protect it from being marked by the bit when it has passed through the metal. The bit should not be pushed through the metal in one go, but just down a little way, brought up and then pushed down again. This stops it from jamming or breaking in the hole, prevents the drill-bit from being blunted, and clears the hole. The drill-bit should be kept lubricated. The metal should be held firmly with fingers out of the way of the drill-bit and chuck. A large hole should be done in two stages – it is drilled with a small bit to open it and then opened out completely with the correctly sized drill.

If the drill does break when in the hole, it should be well oiled and pulled out with pliers. If it cannot be reached, a thin piece of wire should be poked down the hole to push it out. If this fails, the whole piece of metal should be annealed to soften the bit. It then has to be drilled out. If it is impossible to anneal the piece of work, a length of piano wire should be made into a spear drill (see p. 37) and put into a pin vice or hand drill, and the broken drill-bit drilled out, or removed with acid.

Piercing

A piece of metal can be cut out by using a piercing sawframe and blades. These are available in different sizes, depending on the thickness of the metal and the work to be carried out. Simple cutting out is better done with a heavier blade such as a No. 2, and for more intricate work, Nos 5/0 to 8/0 are used. The cutting action

76 Piercing a piece of silver on the bench pin using the piercing sawframe

of the blade is in the downward stroke. The blade is put into the frame, teeth downwards, first by screwing it between the top wing-nut and bolt. The top of the frame is then rested against the pin and the handle against the chest or shoulder, and a gentle pressure is applied. The frame is light, being made from steel and having a wooden handle. As it is springy it gives under pressure. Both hands are thus left free to place the other end of the blade between the bottom wing-nut and bolt. If the pressure is too great the blade will break when the nut is tightened; if it is not strong enough it will be loose and no good for cutting. It should be firm, and 'ping' when plucked. The lines of the design are scribed on to the metal, and holes are drilled in the parts that are to be cut away. A No. 2/0 sawblade is then attached to the top of the sawframe, threaded through the hole and fastened at the bottom of the frame under pressure.

The metal is now ready for cutting. It must be kept flat and steady; if it is knocked or jerked the blade will break. The frame is held upright firmly, but not clasped tightly, and is pulled down, cutting the metal as it goes. As a rhythm is set up hardly any pressure on the frame is needed. Unless it is kept in an upright position, it is easy to undercut the metal, so the other side should constantly be checked to see that it is being cut straight. After the metal has been cut out the bottom wing-nut is undone and the blade threaded through the next hole. When all the holes have been pierced, the metal should be turned over and the blade threaded through the other side of the metal, this time using a thinner blade such as a No. 5/0. The purpose of turning the metal over is to even up the other side which is bound to be less neat than the first side, and to remove a burr that will have formed. After tidying up this side of the metal, the holes can be filed either with very small needle files, or by using a saw-blade. A very fine blade is used for this: 5/0–8/0. The frame is held upright but, instead of the full face of the blade being used to cut the metal, the edge is used rather like a scraper or a file to smooth out the metal. If this is carried out carefully, a very fine finish can be achieved that does not need to be filed, but if a great deal of piercing is to be done, it is often better to polish the work beforehand, finishing it lightly afterwards, as polishing will take the crisp edge off the pierced work.

77 Pierced silver bookmarker. Frances Loyen, 1975

Making screws

Often a job cannot have all its pieces soldered together. If it is to be enamelled, a separate panel has to be made as a complete piece of work can rarely be put into a kiln, firstly because it would warp as a result of being taken quickly to a high temperature and then down to room temperature when brought out of the kiln, and secondly

78 Taps and dies

because only hard and enamelling solder will stand the temperature needed to melt the enamel. Riveting or rub-over settings can be used but they are not always satisfactory. Riveting is not used for enamel work as the enamel is likely to crack when the wire is being hammered. Rub-over settings are useful, but do not always work well on large pieces of work as the fine silver tends to distort when in long thin strips. If neither method is appropriate, screws present a good alternative.

The size of the screw is determined both by the job and by the piece of metal into which it will be screwed. There must be enough metal for strength to be left around the screw after the thread has been cut. When the size of the screw is known, the size of the drill and the wire to make the screw can be checked (see appendix, p. 183). The tools that are needed are taps and dies, which can be bought separately or in sets, the tap making the thread in the hole that has been drilled and the die making the screw, the thread around the wire. There are several types of screws, each with a different thread; some are coarse, giving a long spiral, others fine, giving a small close spiral. The best types of thread for cutting into silver are B. A. (British Association) or a fine metric. Both these have a close thread.

Taps, especially the smaller sizes, can easily be broken and must be used carefully, Beeswax is rubbed on to them for lubrication. The hole is drilled in the metal and the tap fixed in a holder and screwed into the metal, cutting a thread as it goes. It should be turned two or three times, then reversed to clear the hole and prevent it from sticking. This process should be continued until the thread is completed. The tap must be held at right angles to the metal it is entering and, as it is turned, it must be checked on each side to ensure that it is not leaning. The piece of metal, if small enough, must be held firmly in the hand, or else fastened into a vice. Taps are bought in sets of three, one with a taper on it to begin the hole, another to open it out, and a third to take the thread to the bottom of the hole. If the hole is drilled right through the metal, only one of the taps needs to be used.

The screws are made by taking the correct size piece of wire, making sure that it is hard and straight. If it is not, a drawplate must be clamped into a vice and wire threaded through a hole in it. To the end of the wire a small hand-vice should be attached to prevent the wire from being pulled through completely. The wire is then held in the drawtongs, pulled and twisted. This will harden and straighten it. It is then clamped upright in a vice. The die is placed in a holder and screwed on to the wire, cutting a thread on the outside. Again this must be kept upright and straight, and it is touched with beeswax as a lubricant. If the screw is to have a flat head, a cut should be made straight across the end of the wire with a fine sawblade.

Riveting

If one piece of metal is being joined to another piece or to another material and cannot be soldered, the pieces may be riveted together. The ivory handle on a tea-pot is riveted to metal sockets that are soldered to the pot. Some metals such as niobium cannot be soldered under normal workshop conditions, and so must be riveted.

Rivets can be made from either chenier (see p. 106) or wire. They can be soldered on to the piece of precious

79 Raised silver tea-pot with bone handle. Gerald Benney, *c.* 1950

metal and passed right through a hole drilled in the piece to which it is to be secured, or pushed into a hole drilled half way through the other material. A rivet can be passed through both pieces to be joined and secured either side, as in the handle of a coffee-pot.

A rivet which is soldered to a piece of metal on to which another material is to be brought is made from round wire. The hole which is drilled half way into the other material is exactly the same size as the round wire to give as tight a fit as possible. The wire is then cut a little longer than is needed and held in sprung tweezers until it has been soldered upright on to the precious metal. (The faces on these tweezers are sprung together and must be squeezed to be opened.) If the metal is G12 (0.90 mm) or over, a hole can be drilled into it to locate the wire while it is being soldered, using only a small amount of solder. Any excess should be cleaned off or the pieces to be joined will not slot together properly. When soldering a wire to a piece of sheet, the sheet should be heated, thereby letting the wire take the heat from it, as if both are heated the wire will melt. When the metal has been cleaned, the wire is cut to size and the two pieces pushed together.

If the rivet is to be soldered on to one piece of metal and passed straight through another piece, again the round wire should fit tightly into the hole. The pieces are pushed together and, where the wire overlaps the other material, it is cut or filed until it is just slightly proud of

80 Pomander with ivy leaves soldered to tendrils and all riveted to body of box. Wooden door with hinges riveted to it. 5.08 cm high. Frances Loyen, 1975

81 Riveting hammer, box hammer and joint-leveller

the surface. It is then tapped lightly with the flat face of a riveting hammer (a small light hammer with one flat face and the other wedge-shaped) to flatten out the end of the wire by slightly burring the edge and holding the two pieces together. If chenier is used it is filed just proud of the piece, and the tip of a burnisher, scriber or centre-punch is pushed into the centre and rolled around the sides of the chenier, splaying it out slightly. The chenier can also be cut to make four sections. If each of these sections is filed with a round or square needle file, a more decorative effect is achieved.

When the rivet is to pass through the whole job, either chenier or wire can be used. One side is rested against a flat plate while the other is being riveted; then the work is turned over, the other side is rested on the flat plate and the process repeated.

Should a space be needed between two sheets of metal to be fastened together, chenier is soldered on to one sheet and wire of the same size as the hole in the chenier, made to fit as tightly as possible, is soldered on to the other. They are then pushed together. Often it is better to rivet flat sheets of metal together rather than to solder them, as this can distort the metal. Riveting is also used if the flat surface is inaccessible to plates, a stake or a hammer.

All rivets and the heads of screws can be finished off with a grain tool. Normally used in jewellery-making for setting, this is a small piece of steel, which is available in various sizes, with a polished concave hemisphere turned in it. It is held in a ball-shaped handle in the palm of the hand and the end of the tool is fitted over the wire or chenier. It is then rolled around, burnishing and smoothing off the corners of the rivet.

Wire

Wire made from precious metal can be bought in a large range of sizes and shapes, such as round, rectangular, square or half-round, but it is practical and more economical to buy it in a heavy section and reshape or pull it down smaller in the workshop. Often only a short piece of wire is needed, and most bullion dealers have a weight and a price limit below which they will not sell metals. Occasionally a piece of wire is needed that is not a standard size or shape and so must be made. It is not practical to carry a large stock of wire if it is rarely used.

A useful sized wire to buy is 3 mm square section as this can be pulled down to smaller sizes. Unless a great amount of wire over this size is used, it should only be bought when specifically needed.

Rolling mills

These are two sets of rollers, one for sheet and one for wire. Both have a machined finish that should be well looked after. Hardened steel wire should not be put through them or they will mark badly. The surface of the rollers should be greased regularly. The rollers are turned by a handle at one side of the machine, and the space between them can be altered by turning knobs at the top and bottom, bringing the rollers together or apart in a parallel motion. The rollers for sheet have a flat surface and are used for taking down the gauge of metal, making it thinner. The wire rollers consist of two parallel lines of different sized right angles; these move together to make square wire. Reducing the size of the wire is done in stages by rolling the metal through progressively smaller openings until the required size is reached. With both types of roller, the metal must be turned to make sure it is not compressed in one direction only. The wire is put through the same size gap twice, and is turned to ensure that it is evenly rolled. If the sheet is rolled in one direction only, it will stretch in that direction, hardly increasing in width. If a square piece of metal is to be rolled, it must be done in both directions.

If a piece of round wire of small diameter is needed and only larger square wire is in stock, this can be reduced in cross-section by rolling it through the square mills until it is only a little larger than required. It is then pulled down to size through a round-holed drawplate which is a flat steel plate with holes of graduated sizes, and various shapes – round, knife-edge, square, different section half-round, sage-leaf, oval and rectangular. The sizes of the holes range from 0.5 mm upwards. To get the best

82 Rolling mills

use from them a draw-bench (see below) is needed, but some drawing down of wire can be done by putting the plate in a vice. The end of the wire is filed to a taper, and the rest of the piece of wire is warmed and run through a piece of beeswax. The taper is then pushed into the hole nearest its size, grasped with drawtongs, and pulled through. (Drawtongs are heavy iron tongs with serrated faces to grip the wire.) The wire is pulled down to the required size in stages. If it has to pass through several holes the metal must be annealed or it will crack. If the metal needs to be springy and hard when it reaches the last hole, care should be taken to arrange the annealings so that they do not come too near the end of the run.

Annealing wire

Wire should be annealed very carefully and it must be done evenly, which is slightly more difficult than when annealing sheet. It is impossible to draw down 9 carat wire, as it becomes too hard and brittle if not properly annealed. If the wire is heavy, it should be placed on a wire grid on the hearth and the flame run along the length of the wire rather than across it, bringing it up to temperature. If it is annealed across its length only short pieces will be done properly. If the wire is thin it should be wound into a coil and the whole coil, if possible, put into a tobacco tin or something similar, and heated to temperature. Silver should alway be quenched but care must be taken with certain gold alloys as to how they should be cooled: a bullion dealer will give advice on this. They may have to be quenched once the metal has been cooled to black heat (450–500°C). Above this temperature they could crack. Some must be quenched above 500°C as they are age-hardenable, and would harden if cooled below a certain temperature.

Draw-bench

This hand-operated machine has a handle attached to a circular chain, running along a bench, with drawtongs which grip wire and pull it through a drawplate down to a smaller section.

Swage

A swage can be put together to make a wire of a different shape. Take two rectangular blocks of steel about 12 mm thick and drill holes down through them edge to edge. Tap them to the size of a bolt, about 6 mm diameter, so that they can be screwed together. The required shape is then pierced out of each half of the metal so that when they are fitted together the complete shape is formed. The precious metal wire, which must be about a third larger than the required size, is placed between the two pieces of metal. These are screwed up firmly leaving a piece of wire overlapping to be gripped by the drawtongs. It is larger than the hole in the plate and, after it has been pulled through, the plates are tightened together. The wire is pulled through almost completely, leaving half an inch at the other end for the drawtongs to pull it back again. As the wire begins to take shape slowly, it must be annealed often.

Making chenier

To make tubing in the workshop a strip of silver 4 cm wide is filed true and annealed. One end is cut to a point and the metal placed in a swage block with a piece of steel

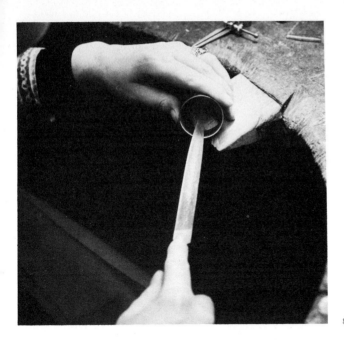

83 Mitring the base of a round box

rod over it which is hammered down into each groove until the edges meet. These are then sprung together and soldered with hard solder, forming a tube which is pulled through a drawplate with round holes to the required size. As the metal is pulled through the plate the inside of the tube becomes smaller, and so a length of piano wire is oiled and inserted. This should be gripped inside the silver tube in the taper and must overlap it at the end. The metal not only reduces in section but lengthens, and if the hardened wire is not long enough the silver wire will overtake it. Chenier made in the workshop, however, is not as satisfactory as ready-made seamless tubing; it will always have a solder line which can split, and if making a hinge with it the solder line must always be placed down into the bearer. Thick-wall chenier can be made by using a heavier gauge metal sheet, such as G20 (1.65 mm).

Making a round box

The most straightforward type of box to make is a round one with a push-fit lid. Take a sheet of silver G12 (0.90 mm) and file it true. Multiply the diameter by $\pi(3\frac{1}{7}$ or 3.14) to obtain the length of the sheet; the width is cut to the required height of the box. The silver is malleted around a parallel stake and soldered to form a cylinder. Any excess solder is filed off and the cylinder returned to the stake to be made round again. The sides are trued up by holding a ruler along the length of the cylinder to see if there are any high or low spots; if so, these are removed as described below.

If the centre is bowed in (smaller than the required diameter), it should be lightly planished out to size: if the ends are splayed out they should be gently malleted on air, resting the body of the cylinder on the stake with the ends overlapping. If the centre is bowed out, two pieces of paper are rested on the stake on either side of the bow, which is sharply struck with a planishing hammer. The metal will go down on to the stake and spring back into the correct position. If the ends of the cylinder taper in they must be carefully planished. Once the box is round and true, one end is placed on a surface plate, the machined steel block, with the engineer's square up against its side and resting on its stock. If the bottom of the cylinder resting on the surface plate is not flat, the cylinder will lean: if it leans away from the square, the high spot is on the edge nearest the square; if it leans towards it, the high spot is on the side opposite. This high spot is filed off across the diameter of the cylinder. It should be checked again. The whole process is repeated, moving the square around the cylinder checking to see if it leans in any direction. The burr must be removed regularly as it will prevent the cylinder from standing upright. When it is erect, the base is ready to be fitted. It can either be mitred into position or butted on. In either case the metal is held on with binding wire hooked over the top edges, the tightening loops fastened at the junction of the base and the cylinder. If it is to be butted into position, stitches 5 mm apart must be cut around the base to prevent it from warping. The cylinder is then ready to be soldered.

The next stage is to straighten the other end in the same way as the first side. When it is ready for the end to be

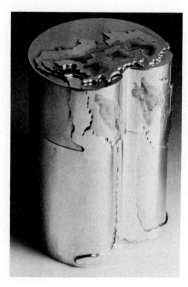

84 Silver box decorated with enamel. Frances Loyen, 1976

85 The same box, showing bezel

86 Scribing block, surface plate and angle plate

soldered in position the depth of the lid must be decided. The cylinder makes up the whole body of the box, the lid being a slice cut off it. The depth of the lid is measured from the newly filed end and it is marked by a short line (about 2 cm in length going around the cylinder), using a scribing block. A sawcut is made along this line to provide the air hole necessary to prevent it from exploding while it is being soldered (see p. 76). Once the end is soldered in position and allowed to cool, the lid is cut off completely along the line made by the scribing block.

Scribing block

This is a square block of steel with an upright rod to which is attached a scriber: the rod can be tilted back and forth, and the scriber adjusted up and down. The cylinder is rested with the newly filed edge (before the second end is soldered into position) on the surface plate and the scriber is adjusted to the right height of the lid. The cylinder is slowly turned and the scriber will mark the correct position. Once the cylinder has been cut in two the new raw ends are filed true, using the surface plate and engineer's square in the same way as for the ends of the cylinder. The lid and bottom should fit together so that the line is barely visible.

Bezel

This is a collar of metal soldered to the inside of the box to hold the lid in position. It must fit inside exactly. Measurements are taken and a strip of metal cut to size and filed true is malleted around a stake and soldered. Then a line is scribed around the inside of the box and stitches taken down to it. The bezel is pushed down on to the stitches and held in place with cotter-pins. The size of the bezel depends on the box: it must overlap the top of the box enough to hold the lid firmly and reach down into the box sufficiently to support itself. The bezel on a round box approximately 5 cm in diameter by 10 cm in height would reach about 6 mm into the box. If it is too long the lid will be difficult to fit down on to the box. After the bezel has been soldered it can be filed down if too high and, if the lid still does not fit, the top edge of the bezel should be carefully malleted over a stake to turn in slightly. Alternatively the top edge can be filed off so that it just tapers a bit.

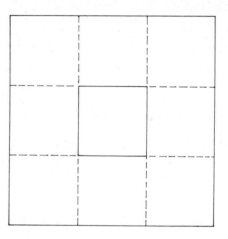

87 Development of a square box. The dotted lines are cut and the sides folded, in this case to form a cube. A separate sheet, filed up and with the edges mitred, is then soldered on to form the sixth side

Square box with a hinge

The shell of the box is made up of two pieces, one for the top panel and sides and the other for the bottom panel or base. The size of the sheet of metal is calculated by taking the plan view and adding the depth as a perimeter. If a box is to be 8 cm × 8 cm and 5 cm deep, a sheet of metal 18 cm × 18 cm is needed. G12 can be used for silver and G11 for gold. The sheet is squared up.

The depth (5 cm) is scribed in from the edge of the sheet of metal on all four sides and the lines are then cut with a scoring tool; if the sides are to be upright a cutting angle of 90° is needed. The tool is held and drawn along each of the scribed lines in turn at the correct cutting angle. Scoring must be done accurately, evenly and methodically. If one line is cut more deeply than the others the angle will not be 90°; if the tool is tipped to one side the corner of the box will not be straight. When a thin impression of the line is just visible on the other side of the

88 Scoring a piece of silver

metal the process is completed. Before the metal can be folded the small squares formed at each corner of the metal are cut out with a sawframe along the lines made by the scoring tool, and the metal on either side of the scored line should be cleaned ready for soldering before the box is folded.

The metal is now rested on a small flat stake and the sides folded over. It is bound and soldered with hard solder (the binding wire is wrapped round the sides of the box, the tightening loops at each corner). Metal strips such as the thin steel U-section strips found in umbrellas can be annealed and fitted on to the top edges of the box to prevent them from warping. The box should not be quenched as it will distort, and when it has cooled it must be trued up, preferably by *plating*. The sides of a scored box with flat sides must always be filed flat or, when it is polished, the surface will be rippled and the box will look dented. If the metal is uneven before it is filed, this will show along the top edge after it has been filed and at the corners, which will be filed too thin.

Truing up a box by plating

Plating is a method of truing up a box and making the sides flat, as well as a way of flattening metal. The plates are made from iron sheet about 3 mm thick. If a sheet of metal is to be flattened it is clamped between two of these plates cut either to size or a little bigger than the metal. G-clamps are used with a narrow strip of steel between the plate and the screw of the clamp to spread out the pressure so that a mark is not left on the metal. The clamps are screwed up tightly and the whole piece heated to a dark even red. It is then left to cool completely and when the plates are removed the metal is flat. Plating a box works on the same principle. Plates are cut to fit the sides, bottom and top of the box; then they are fitted inside and out clamped together and heated. This method is not often used on 'one-off' boxes as it does take some time to make the plates: the result, however, is much better than any other way of straightening a box and it is a good idea gradually to build up a collection of plates.

Truing up a box by hand and hammer

The other method of truing up a box is to use the fingers and a planishing or box hammer. It is very easy to stretch the metal when hammering the box, thus distorting it, and often when this is done, the process cannot be reversed, so the hammer should be used as little as possible. The box is held up to the light with an engineer's square to see that all the corners are at right angles to each other. If they are not the box is rested on its side and pushed down or malleted lightly on one of its corners until it becomes square. If the sides splay out at the ends they must be malleted on air. A piece of wood is used to support the bulk of the box on the inside, leaving the offending side overlapping. This is then malleted on air. If a side bows in at the centre, it should be pushed outwards with the fingers or lightly planished out. If the end bows in, it must also be pushed or planished out. Should the base bow in, the box can be placed, base downwards, on a stake resting on two pieces of paper on either side of the bow, and pushed down with the fingers or with a planishing hammer. The metal can often be burnished by being rubbed back and forth over a stake, constant pressure being maintained, instead of being hammered. It can also be hammered from the back on a stake, although if not done carefully the metal may be stretched, thus pushing the sides out.

Once the box is square and the sides true it is placed on a surface plate and the top edge is measured with the scribing block, so that the high spots can be filed off, leaving an even surface. When it is even it is turned upside down and tested against an engineer's square.

When the top edge has been filed down it should be mitred (see p. 96) on each side, and a sheet of metal is cut to size and also mitred to fit it. The height of the lid is now measured with the scribing block and a cut made for the air hole. The panel is then soldered into position with hard solder and the top is cut off the box. The two pieces of the box must again be trued up in case they have warped while being soldered, and the ends are filed true so that the two parts fit together with the line between them hardly showing.

Thickening wires can now be made for the box; although they are not essential, they give a thick edge to the box, making it look more substantial and adding

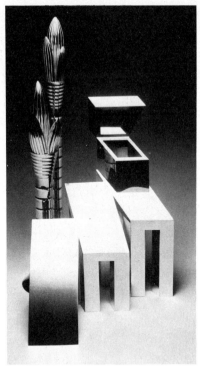

weight to it. They are necessary, however, if a spring and push clasp is to be fitted. The size of the wire used depends on the size of the box. It is usually rectangular and is fitted into the box and lid, just proud of the top edge, to which it is then filed down. For a box size 8 cm × 8 cm × 5 cm, rectangular wire is used (1.5 mm × 2.5 mm) filed down to 1.5 mm square. The inside length of the box is transferred on to the wire with dividers and an angle cut at the ends with a square needle file, to mitre them together. The wire is filed only to make up three sides, as it is not needed on the side holding the hinge. Each corner is filed, leaving a wafer of metal, thus enabling it to be folded without coming apart. It is soldered with hard solder. A line is scribed 1.5 mm down from the top edge of the box and the same just inside the lid, and stitches are taken down to each of these lines. The wires are rested on the stitches and held in position with cotter-pins. They are then soldered. After being pickled the wire is filed down to the level of the top edge of the box.

Making a folded box

Another way of forming a box is by hammering it over a steel block. The size of the sheet of metal is worked out but instead of the complete depth of the box being added

91 Folding the side of a box

to the perimeter of the sheet, only half the height is added. The top and bottom are made in separate pieces so two sheets of metal are needed. Lines are scribed around the edges of the metal indicating the sides of the box, and the small squares formed at each corner of the sheet are cut out as on the scored box. The general shape of this type of box is different from the scored box as the edges and corners are slightly rounded instead of being sharp.

A steel block is made to the dimensions of the box; the edges do not have to be rounded, but they may be slightly softened for if they are too sharp the edge of the block will cut into the precious metal. As the block does not have sharp 90° angles at its corners, the precious metal must be filed so that when it is folded the corners will go together with the same rounded angle as that of the corner of the steel block. This angle is roughly 30°, although once the metal has been folded its angle can be fitted properly by a sawcut between the two sides of the corner.

The precious metal is annealed, sandwiched between the steel block and another sheet of steel 3 mm thick, and fastened into a vice. The perimeter of the sheet of metal which will form the sides of the box is left standing above the steel block, the line showing its depth being in line with the top of the steel block. This metal is now bent over flat against the steel block, a piece of wood being hammered against it to bring it over, preventing it from becoming thin or having hammer marks cut into its surface. Each side is folded in turn, and when they have all been folded into the right position and checked with an engineer's square, they can be soldered at the corners. Both top and bottom are made the same way and then filed to fit each other.

Hinges

There are several different sorts of hinges, but the basic methods of putting them together may be illustrated when either gate hinges or flush hinges are made. A hinge is made up of chenier cut into 'knuckles' and soldered into two bearer wires, one of which has been soldered into the lid, the other into the box. The size of the joint depends on the design of the box; an 8 cm × 8 cm box can take a hinge of 1.5 mm diameter chenier soldered into two 1.5 mm bearer wires, or equally well a larger chenier in larger wires. A 20 cm × 10 cm box would need 3 mm chenier in two 3 mm bearers for an adequately strong joint.

The bearer wires are cut to size: in this case they are cut to fit inside a 5 cm × 5 cm box, so they must be 5 cm long, less the thickness of the metal of the box. The measurement should be taken with dividers. The ends of the wire must be filed off square, fitted just inside the top and bottom of the box on stitches and held in place by cotter-pins; they are then soldered, using hard solder. They must now be gapped out to take the chenier. A line is scribed in the centre along the length of the wire and cut with a graver. It is widened slightly with a three-square needle file in order to locate the gapping file, which is a round parallel file, the size for this box being 1.5 mm. The wire is filed evenly along its length. It must be checked regularly with a ruler and by eye to see that it has neither dropped in the middle nor leans more one way than the other. It must also be checked to see that it is not veering across the wire. A piece of steel of the same size as the chenier is used to check the gapping, since it is a stronger metal than silver and will stay straight. Silver chenier might bend if it is constantly picked up and put down.

If the chenier is bent slightly it can be straightened if it is placed between two flat stakes and rolled. Hammering could cause it to collapse and would dent the surface, making it unusable.

The gapping is done to the lid and the bottom of the box at the same time. The steel rod is put between them at intervals, and when the two sides are gapped evenly (0.75 mm on each side) and fit together, the gapping is finished. The chenier should move to and fro when put between the bearers, but should lock if pressure is put on the box.

With the steel rod in position and the bearers properly gapped, the box will not open and so an angle must be

92 Silver box, hinged lid with mother of pearl. Frances Loyen, 1979

93 Clamps holding bearer wire in position before soldering

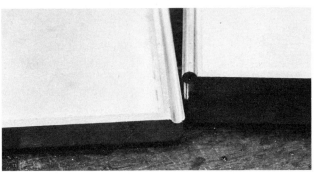

94 Gapped bearer wire showing chenier in position

filed on the back edge of the box. The angle depends on the design of the box, but the most usual one is 45° on both sides. It is filed on the back edge of the bearer towards the bottom of the box on the outside. A small angle is filed down equally along the bearer on both the lid and the bottom of the box, and the two sides are put together again. The lid is opened to see how far it will go, taken apart and filed again. The lid is continually tested in this way until it opens upright. It should not be allowed to open more than 90° as the pressure may break the hinge, known as a gate hinge.

The bezel should now be made by measuring the length of each of the sides of the box, excluding the side with the bearer wires, and transferring them on to a strip of silver. The corners are mitred with a square needle file and soldered with hard solder. The whole bezel is soldered into position against the thickening wires with hard solder held in position with cotter-pins or steel clamps.

Knuckles

To make the knuckles of the joint the chenier must be cut. The number of knuckles in a box is always uneven, normally five or seven unless a spring hinge is made. Most of the knuckles are put on the lid giving it more support; an object jammed in the box would otherwise cause the lid to distort.

The knuckles are cut with the help of a joint leveller, a flat machined piece of hardened steel about 2.5 mm thick. It has a triangular hole with a screw leading into it from the top end of the tool. The chenier is put in the hole, slightly proud of the surface of the metal and the screw tightened, which holds it in place. A file is run straight across the metal bringing it down to the surface of the tool, giving it an accurate face, square to the rest of the chenier. The length of each knuckle is worked out and the measurement transferred with dividers, marking a scribed line on the chenier. It is again put in the tool (the scribed line on a level with the face of the tool) and is cut off. It is then filed down to the face of the tool. Each knuckle is cut separately in this way, and as each one is cut the burr must be carefully filed off. Only the burr must be touched; if the corner of the chenier is broken it will result in a badly fitting hinge. All the knuckles are cut the same size except the two end ones which must overlap the box slightly, to be filed flush later.

The knuckles are put on a piece of straight steel wire and positioned along the bearers. They must be pushed together tightly so that there are no gaps between them. A small paillon of easy solder dipped in borax is placed on each knuckle, alternately on the lid and on the bottom of the box, the end ones being on the lid. The object is to

95 Knuckles in a box for a gate hinge

make the solder tack the knuckles in place. If they were done in the normal way, the solder would run and the joint would stick together in a solid lump. The box is heated gently to allow the borax to bubble up and settle again; any paillon that jumps out of position should be pushed back into line. It is useful to have a long steel needle with blunt ends for prodding jobs like this. When the box reaches the correct temperature the paillon will suddenly flush and the flame must be pulled away immediately. When the box has cooled it is not yet put in the pickle. The two sides are pulled apart and every knuckle is bound separately around the box, the tightening loops resting on top of each one. The spaces between the knuckles are painted with rouge powder and water to stop the solder running into them. The solder is then flushed properly and drawn under the knuckles to attach them securely to the bearers. The box is then pickled and every knuckle checked; if there is not enough solder, the joint is scraped with a scriber, boraxed, bound and more solder is added. The box is not pickled after the knuckles are first tacked into position as the sulphuric acid would stop the solder running at the next stage.

It is likely that the two sides will not fit together easily. They must be carefully manipulated into position using a little beeswax. If, however, they do not go down flat into position the cause may be a minute piece of solder which may only be seen through an eye-glass, yet may be large enough to damage the knuckles. It should be carefully removed with a graver. The knuckles should be treated with great care: they should be firmly attached but excess solder can damage the edge of a knuckle and cause a gap in the joint. Too much pulling and pushing apart of a good tight hinge will burnish the corners, and leave ugly gaps. It should not be opened or close unneccessarily until it has been pinned together.

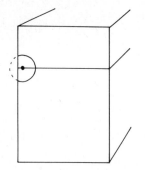

96 Flush hinge showing amount of chenier that has to be filed off the back

97 Silver cigarette box with a flush hinge, scored, folded and soldered. Frances Loyen, 1975

Flush hinge

A larger chenier is used in this hinge than in others. The effect is of a flat side where the hinge would normally show, and it is seen only when the lid is opened and the knuckles are moved. The bearers for a box 8 cm × 8 cm (or any size up to 20 cm × 10 cm) are 3 mm square. They are soldered into position as for the gate hinge and then gapped. The lid and bottom of the box are held together, and the position of the hole in the chenier must be visualized as it cannot be marked. The idea is to gap out the bearer far enough back to break through the back edge of the box, leaving one side of the knuckles sticking out. Later the knuckles are filed flush with the rest of the box, and the hole in the chenier must be far enough in so as not to wear through the back edge that has been filed. If it is too far in, the box will not open properly. It is a good idea to draw a side view of the box and hinge, laying a tracing of the hinge and lid over it. A pin is put through the paper into the hole in the chenier and the tracing is moved round as if the lid were being opened. It is thus possible to see where the hinge should be placed.

A line is scribed along the bearers, off centre, nearer the back edge. It is opened out as for the gate hinge, but this must be done even more carefully as the gapping file is large, and the gapping is done to the back edge of the box as well as to the bearer wires. Once the chenier is soldered into position the hinge is pinned up before the knuckles are filed flush with the back of the box. If the knuckles do not fit the bearer correctly or if an excess solder has been used, small pin-holes will appear along the joint. This defect can only be disguised if the box is to be textured or engine-turned.

98 Silver tea-pot with ivory handle, flush-hinged lid. Robert Welch, c. 1960

99 Silver box with a flush hinge and pin holding it together

Pinning up

This is the operation of putting the pin into the hinge to hold it together. The first pin that is used can be made from nickel silver or hardened steel; it is used to hold the box together while it is being filed and is removed after polishing when the final pin is put in. The pin should fit the hole in the chenier tightly. If nickel silver is used it must be pulled down through a drawplate until it is hard (hard-drawn). A taper is filed in the end of the pin which must be straight, rubbed with beeswax and put in either a hand drill or a pin vice. It is then pushed into the hole and turned gently as if being *screwed* in. The pin must always be turned in that direction except if it is being pulled out, when it must be turned as if it is being *unscrewed*, and gently pulled at the same time. If it should stick, it must not be forced or it will break in the joint; it should be moved gently back and forth, being turned carefully.

When the box has been polished (it must always be polished with a pin in it), the pin is removed. The final pin is put into its place, and should only reach half way along the end knuckles, leaving a small gap at either end. It is pushed into place, laid on its side and gently tapped into position using a hammer and a small steel tool such as a centre-punch. Care should be taken not to hammer the end knuckle, thereby distorting it. When the steel pin is in position two small pieces of tight fitting silver wire are pushed into each end of the hinge and riveted carefully with a hammer. The ends are then filed and polished. A silver pin is not used as it will wear quickly or break in the knuckles. If a pin should jam or snap inside the hinge and cannot be removed, a piano wire spear drill must be made to remove it. If the steel pin is too hard to be drilled out, the whole piece should be put in the sulphuric acid (the pickle) and left over-night to dissolve the pin. A box must never be annealed with the pin in it as the pin would soften and jam with the chenier as well as possibly distort the box.

Spring joint

This is made in the same way as either a gate hinge or a
flush hinge, except that an even number of knuckles is
used. Both ends of the steel pin are filed flat. The pin is
pushed into position, and must be long enough to overlap
the end of the box by 5 mm. The lid of the box is closed
while being pinned up and one end of the wire is trapped
flat with a wedge of silver (or gold) wire. The lid of the
box is opened and the other end of the wire is then
trapped. If the lid is heavy or more spring is required, the
pin should be twisted after the lid has been opened before
being trapped. The size of the hole in the chenier which
rules the size of the pin should vary according to the box.
It is unnecessary to have a large hole in the chenier of a
small box, nor is a bezel necessary on a box with a spring
hinge; instead it may have a catch, a 'spring and push' to
hold the lid closed.

Spring catch

A spring and push catch is made as follows. A hole is
drilled centre front of the bottom half of the box below
the thickening wire and a 'button' is filed out of sheet or
wire to fit into it. The button can be any shape, round or
square, a long thin bar, but the hole must cut to the shape
of the button which must fit it exactly. It must be at least
three times the thickness of the gauge of the metal used
for the box; there must be enough metal to pass through
the box and to push the spring far enough in to release the
catch which holds the lid closed. The spring can be made
from any hard, springy material such as titanium, monel
or sprung steel; it is a narrow piece of flat sheet, and for a
box 2.5 cm deep with a button or push 1.5 cm × 3 mm a
strip approximately 6 cm × 5 mm G20 (1.65 mm) is
needed. The strip is cut into an inverted 'T' shape; the
piece going across will act as the spring, the upright as the
clip to hold the box closed. The width of the spring and
also the upright or clip should be 3 mm. The clip must
hook over the thickening wire on the lid and rather than
bending the end of the clip over, giving it a tinny look, the
spring is filed down to about G9 (0.60 mm), leaving a
small ridge (about 1.5 mm wide) to act as a clip at the top
of the upright section. That is why G20 is used; it is far
too heavy to use as a spring unless filed down. G9 cannot
be used because a clip would have to be soldered on to it,
thus taking the spring out of the metal.

Two boxes, called 'goal posts', are made to fit the
spring and hold it in position. They are made to the same
width as the spring, 3 mm in this case, and should be
about 4.5 mm in length. Two strips each 1 cm × 5 mm
are filed true. They are divided into three sections each
3 mm wide, scored (i.e. filed with a square needle file),

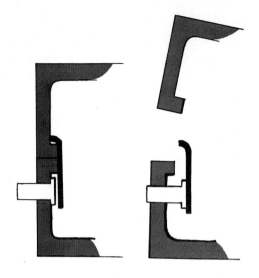

100 Spring and push, showing action of button on spring

folded and soldered. The height is filed down to take the spring tightly. They are then filed to the correct length (4.5 mm) and soldered into position. If the spring is 6 cm in length the goal posts must be just over 6 cm apart. The spring must lie flat in position with no movement in any direction.

It will be noted that at this point the spring cannot lie flat because the thickening wire is in the way. A line should be scribed on each side of the spring metal where it passes over the thickening wire (about half its width only) with a square needle file. The same must be done to the thickening wire in the lid although care must be taken not to file too much off as this wire holds the clip in position.

A small piece of sheet must now be soldered on to the back of the push or button, larger than the hole through which it is pushed to operate the spring. When this has been done the button is pushed through the hole from the inside of the box, the sheet previously soldered on to it

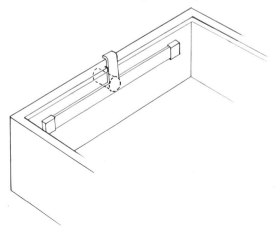

101 Complete view of spring and push

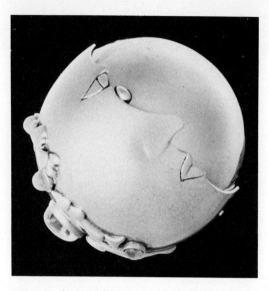

102 Silver box set with moonstones.
Frances Loyen, 1976

preventing it from falling out, and the spring is first slotted into one goal post, bent slightly and then pushed into the other. It will spring flat holding the button firmly in position.

Another way of opening a box with a spring hinge is by squeezing it, but this can only be done if the box is round, oval or spherical. A 'nib', which is a small piece of sheet about 1.5 mm in width with a bit of round wire soldered on to one end of it, is rounded off on all sides and soldered to the inside of the lid. The measurement of the length of the nib is transferred to the inside of the box at the front and a small recess is cut into the metal with a graver at the point where the nib is positioned when the lid is closed. The lid will spring open when the box is squeezed, the metal being distorted slightly and so releasing the catch. It will not work, however, if the box has thickening wires.

If a box does not have a spring catch a spring can be put inside it. Again the box must be round, oval, or spherical with no thickening wires. A nib is soldered to the front as a catch. Inside the box, on the same side as the hinge, and going down into the box two goal posts are soldered, one through which the spring is to be threaded, and the other (which is four-sided) to prevent the spring from slipping through. These are positioned at the bottom of the inside of the box and half way up it. The spring should be made from any suitable material such as steel or titanium, and filed into a strip long enough to fold over into an 'S' shape which will be wedged against the lid. When the box is squeezed the nib will be released and the spring will force the lid open. The spring can be filed or pierced to a decorative shape as long as it is not made too narrow at any point, and if titanium or niobium is used it can be coloured by anodic oxidization.

A shell of a box can be made by many different techniques, such as hammering, folding, casting and repoussé work. An oval box is made in the same way as a round one but instead of the malleting being done around a parallel stake it is done around an oval one. If the box is shallow, up to about 2.5 cm, the silver sheet can be wrapped around a 3 mm iron plate cut to the right shape and size, instead of making a heavy steel stake. The precious metal must fit around the plate particularly well because the lid on an oval box must fit without a hinge.

Once the shell of a box is made, the two edges must fit together perfectly before the hinge can be fitted. When they have been filed to make a good fit, they must be rubbed on to the surface plate. This will serve to burnish the high spots, which can then be seen and filed off. With most boxes formed by repoussé work or casting, thickening wires must be added.

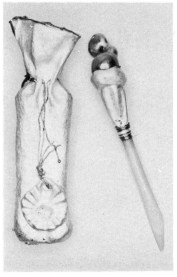

103 Toothpick and case in silver, red, gold and baroque pearl. Diana Hobson, 1977

Use of other materials

If a box is to have any metal or material added which cannot be soldered, another way of 'bringing it on' must be found. For a precious or semi-precious stone rivets or screws would in most cases be impossible, or would spoil the look of the piece, so a setting is made to hold it. If the whole of the lid of the box is to be covered by the stone then the box is made in the usual way, but without adding the final panel. Instead, a wire is soldered inside the box below the top edge and the stone is dropped on to this. The setting is done by filing a little of the thickness from the sheet of the main body. The metal is pushed over, wedging the stone in position by using a short piece of steel wire 3 mm square with softened corners, pushed into a small round handle which is held in the palm of the hand. The metal is pushed inwards with the tool at intervals at opposite sides, until all the metal has been pushed over the stone. The metal is then burnished flat and filed smooth. If the stone is a flat slice the metal need only be pushed inwards slightly to jam it in position and need not overlap the top of the stone.

If the box is to have a stone brought on to it and has to have a separate setting made, fine silver or fine gold are used. The setting is made as a flat strip (G8 – 0.55 mm), which is fitted tightly around the outside edge of the stone, removed and then soldered. It should stand the same height as the stone, if the stone is flat, or just reach to where the stone begins to fall away if it is rounded (a cabochon cut). This setting is soldered on to the main body of the box, with stitches to hold it in place. The setting is again done by pushing the metal over, but, as it is fine silver rather than standard, the metal is much softer and easier to manipulate.

104 Hand-forged silver spoons. William Phipps, 1970

9 Cutlery – wire hammering, stamping and pressing

When precious metal wire is run through the square holes of a set of rolling mills (see p. 104) it will increase in length. In the same way when metal is hammered it will stretch only in the direction in which it is being hammered; a piece of wire hammered across its width will increase in width. It is this principle that is used for hammer work of any sort, whether it be forging, raising or flattening metal. Hammering a piece of heavy copper wire (e.g. 3 mm diameter) will show how the principle works, and how easily the metal stretches and can be shaped.

Spoon-making is a highly skilled job, the spoons being forged from a heavy piece of wire, the size depending on the size of the spoon, although it is possible to cut corners by using cross-rolled blanks that can be bought from a bullion dealer. These consist of heavy gauge silver wire that has been rolled out in length and then rolled across at one end, splaying the metal out into the form of an exaggerated flat spoon. They must be stamped into lead or a die or rolled through a set of special rollers to form

105 Hammering metal across surface to stretch it widthways

106 Silver bowl peened from a small thick blank. Frances Loyen, 1975

the bowl shape. (This is done only if large quantities are to be produced.)

Peening

The blank for a spoon was once cast between two steel plates holding between them a piece of steel wire bent to the shape of the bowl of the spoon with a small tang at the top, which would eventually form the handle of the spoon, and also act as a lead-in for when the molten silver was poured into the mould. The blank would be small and thick, and from it the whole spoon would be forged. The method of forming a shallow piece from a small flat sheet of a thick gauge is called 'peening'. The centre of the metal is hammered in circles leading to the outside edge of the blank which, as it is not touched, will not stretch a great deal in width, as well as remaining thick. The rest of the blank is held in tongs and is struck with a full-faced hammer on to a steel plate. The metal is thus pinched between the steel block and the hammer, and so stretched. As the dimensions of the outside edge stay almost the same, the metal must stretch in the only direction it can to form a dish or bowl shape. A shallow dish can be formed in this way by using a smaller thicker blank than would be used if the piece were to be raised. If a deeper form is required with straight sides then the same technique can be followed, the sides being raised in and planished to give more height to the piece.

Spoons

Although silver is the second most malleable metal and can be forged cold, it is quicker, once the skill has been practised, to forge the metal hot. A piece of silver wire, called an ingot, is used to make a spoon, 1.9×4 mm approximately for a tablespoon, 9 mm × 3 mm for a teaspoon. The length will depend on the required size of the spoon.

The tools used are a spoon-maker's teist, a heavy steel plate with a softened, cushioned face, and a forging hammer, a short-headed hammer, weighing about 1.5 kg, one face flat and squat, the other tapered slightly and squat. The metal is held in a pair of tongs with short flat jaws. A lead cake and a punch the shape of the spoon bowl are also needed. The lead cake can be made by melting scraps of lead in a crucible and pouring them into a cake tin, removing the cake from the tin when the metal has cooled. The punch can be bought separately or in a set of different sized punches; they resemble end-stakes, the head being the same shape as the spoon bowl. They can also be made by filing up a heavy piece of steel or brass, making sure that there is enough metal to take pressure without distorting the edge of the face when the tool is hammered into the lead block. This punch or 'dab', as it is sometimes called, should be brazed on to a steel shank to make it easier to use.

The punch must be hammered into the lead cake to form a recess into which the bowl of the spoon can be punched. This recess can also be formed by pouring molten lead around the punch. The working face of the tool should be painted with whiting or rouge powder and water, and suspended over a cake tin. The lead is poured into the tin until it just covers the working surface of the tool which is removed when the lead has cooled.

The edges and the corners of the ingot are filed off to soften them. A mark is made on the metal to indicate how much metal is to be hammered out. For a teaspoon, a mark is made approximately 3.2 cm from the end. The metal is held in the tongs, heated to a dull red and then hammered on to the edge of the teist, behind the mark on the metal that indicates the end of the bowl, striking the metal on its narrow side to 'neck' it in.

The bowl is then hammered to shape, still on the corner of the teist. The object is to hammer the bowl end of the ingot to make it as wide as possible; so it should be hammered across the face of the ingot, not along it. The corners of the bowl are rounded, the bowl held flat on the teist and peened along the middle in a straight line: the whole action is done quickly before the metal can cool. The metal is heated again to a dull red; the handle and more of the bowl are forged out. After being worked and annealed approximately three times the bowl and handle should be almost to size, although the bowl will not be domed properly and there will be no curve to the handle yet. At this stage the bowl only should be annealed and the handle forged hard, as it will need more strength and spring. Once hammered to size, the bowl and handle should be cleaned up with a file. A thin piece of paper is

107–10 Forging the bowl of a spoon

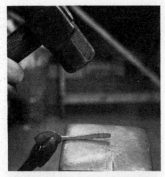

111–12 Forging the handle of a spoon

113–14 Using a punch and lead cake when making a spoon

now smoothed into the recess in the lead cake to protect the precious metal. Every time a lead cake is used, paper should be put between the precious metal and the lead, and the precious metal should always be checked afterwards for specks of lead on its surface.

The handle of the spoon is bent back to an angle of approximately 45°, the bowl is placed over the recess in the lead, the handle hanging over the edge, and the punch is struck down into the recess several times with a hammer. The handle of the spoon will automatically spring up into the correct angle, approximately 12°. The spoon is finally filed up.

If the design of the bowl and handle is intricate, the spoon may have to be made in two parts. The bowl must then be shaped separately in the lead cake, and the handle formed and soldered on afterwards. It will have to be hammered in order to harden it, or hardenable silver can be used.

Forks

The process of forging forks is similar to that used for spoons. Silver wire is used (4.5 mm × 3 mm is a good size). The handle is heated to a dull red and forged to shape. It should only be heated once as it must be given a hard finish. Then the whole piece is forged to shape, the prongs cut with a piercing saw, filed with a needle file, and the fork is bent to shape over a mandrel. If several forks are to be forged, a template should be made for the prongs.

Knives

Silver table knives are usually made with silver handles only, the blades being made from stainless steel and bought separately. A solid handle would be too heavy and so most knife-handles are made hollow, being stamped in two halves and soldered together. This hollow handle is filled with cutler's cement or pitch, and the tang of the knife blade is pushed into it.

Silver fruit knives are often forged from one piece of silver, having a silver blade. They are forged cold, being annealed only once at the start of the process. A stubby ingot is used, a piece of wire approximately 6 mm × 12 mm. The whole knife is made from one ingot, since soldering on a separate silver blade would soften the metal, as well as being unnecessary work. If the two parts are made separately and soldered together, because the design of the knife demands it, then the blade must be hardened afterwards by hammering. Hardenable silver can be used, but as it is a higher grade of silver, it is slightly more expensive. The process of hardening by heating it for several hours in a kiln will also add to the cost.

115 Ingots showing different stages of forging a spoon

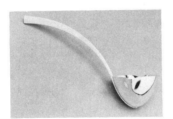

116 Alveston cutlery designed for production in quantity. Robert Welch, 1963

117 Silver punch ladle. The bowl was raised and the handle soldered on after being forged to shape. Susan Fortune, 1978. Photo Ian Dawson

118 Set of silver cutlery. Lindsey Middleton, 1970

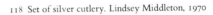

Stamping

Stamping and pressing are closely linked in that they are both done by machinery that forms the metal by compressing it into a former or die, and both are techniques used to produce pieces in quantity. Stamping is done in a mould in one action, considerable force being applied from above the metal. Two precise matched dies are fitted to the machine, one to the base, the other to the head or ram. They are perfectly aligned so that when the weight is dropped, the metal to be formed is compressed and shaped, fitting into the two parts.

A stamping machine is made up of a cast-iron bed to which the lower die is bolted; the upper die (or force) is fitted to the ram which is guided down on upright parallel bars. The two dies slot into each other, the convex shape being the force attached to the ram and the concave die attached to the bed. The metal used to make

119 Fly-press

120 Silver box with fish design struck on a panel and set into the lid. Karina Payne, 1976

the convex die is soften than that used for the concave one, e.g. lead, brass or steel. To operate the machine the ram is guided to the top, the precious metal placed on top of the die on the bed and the ram released. The metal is compressed into the lower die.

Pressing

Pressing is done in a number of actions, the force being slowly exerted several times, compressing the metal into the die. A fly-press is made up of a cast-iron bed with a cast-iron arm extending up and over it. A bolster is attached to the bed to hold the die in position. The cast-iron arm holds the screw-housing and supports for the press ram. The screw-housing holds the leading screw to which are attached the ram-bit at one end (the lower) and a t-bar at the other. The t-bar has either two weights, or one weight and, attached to it, a handle which is swung round, sending the ram down to the bed. It takes several blows to form a piece on a fly-press. These are available in different sizes (see p. 22).

121 Striking

There are many jobs that can be done by stamping or pressing: striking, as in forming coins or medals; blanking, which is cutting out shapes; embossing, which will give an effect resembling chased or repoussé work; forming (see p. 134) and drawing, which is a method of forming deep narrow articles such as pen cases. Work can also be assembled by riveting.

The mass production of complicated stamping and pressing operations will bring down the cost of making an article, but for a small workshop producing pieces only in very small quantities the cost of having dies made may prove too expensive. The quality of the work produced depends on the quality of the die, since the surface of the die is being transferred exactly on to the surface of the precious metal. Die-sinking is a highly skilled job, and complex dies must be made by a professional die-sinker who will carve the metal for the press tool, using scorpers and chisels, leaving as good a finish as possible on the tool.

Simple tools can be made in the workshop, however, and the pieces stamped out not necessarily being the finished article. Knife-handles, spouts and small articles can be made and soldered to a piece of work. Parts of a job, such as two halves of an oval box, can be made and these can be soldered together. Hinges, wires, castings or any decoration may be added later. A simple form, such as a cylinder, can be made into a box of a very different shape – the sides can be faceted in the press, the base and top stamped and soldered on afterwards. Pressing is thus useful in a small workshop to save time on pieces where spinning would be impossible and casting not practical. It should be remembered also that cast pieces do not have the finish or strength of wrought metal.

Making a simple die

The principle of the tool for the spoon being hammered into the lead cake can be used for making a simple press tool. Depending on the shape required, the tool can be made in three different ways. It can be made in the same way as the spoon tool, a piece of metal being filed to shape, coated with whiting and the face cast in lead. In this case it should have a flat back and be brazed on to a flat steel plate to which a short steel shank is attached, screwed or brazed.

Another method is to carve the complete form of the tool out of wood and have it cast in iron, but this is not done if there are any undercuts on the tool, since forming with such an implement would be impossible. A shank is brazed on to this iron tool. A third method is to carve half the tool in wood, if it has undercuts, and have it cast. Once this tool has been cast it should be soldered on to a flat steel sheet with a short shank attached to it.

122 Mustard pot. The body was struck in two halves and soldered together. Jocelyn Burton, 1977

From these tools the die can be made from lead. The complete tool should be placed in the ram, and a heavy steel frame, four sides soldered to a flat steel plate, placed directly under it. The working face of the tool, painted with whiting and water, should sit inside the frame so that it will just be immersed when the lead is poured into the frame. The frame should be wide enough to give approximately 4 cm clearance for the tool on each side, and 4 cm from the bottom of the tool to the base plate of the mould.

The second type of mould for the half-form is made by painting the tool with whiting and water before the shank and back-plate are soldered on to it. The tool is placed flat side down on a steel plate and a steel frame is put over it. Casting sand is packed around the junction of the sides of the steel frame with the base plate to seal it. The molten lead is poured into the mould, allowed to cool slightly and then topped up, so that it is flat. The tool is removed by turning the mould upside down and taking off the steel plate, detaching it from the lead. A back-plate and shank are then soldered on to it. If a deep-stamping is to be done, several moulds should be made, each deeper than the last, the form taking shape gradually. Drawing cannot be done by this method. Lead is very soft and the edges of the tool will wear quickly after stamping only one or two pieces, depending on the shape of the die and its depth. A product called Flexane, made by Devcon, can

123 Simple die. One half of a box, lead cake. The tool is not soldered on to a shank, but placed on top of the precious metal and a tool brought down to it, pushing it into the lead cake

be used in the same way as lead. This is an epoxy resin that dries very hard, yet has a certain give in it. It will stand more working than lead, but, if a large number of pieces are to be stamped, then there is no substitute for a steel tool made by a die-sinker.

Forming the precious metal

The tool will now fit the die exactly, making no clearance for the precious metal that is to be pressed into it. Lead that is being worked will compress and harden, but a newly cast lead cake will give easily. A thin piece of copper (G7–0·50 mm) big enough to overlap the top edge of the mould is annealed, laid over the bottom die and pressed into the mould. The pressing is done in several stages by swinging the t-bar at the top of the machine which pushes the tool attached to the ram down into the die, gradually compressing the metal into it. As the copper is so thin it may crease and, if this happens, it should be removed from the die, malleted flat on a stake and returned to the die. When it fits into the die exactly the top edge should be malleted flat. The purpose of this copper lining is to protect the precious metal from the lead. This need not be done if Flexane is used.

To stretch the mould in order to give enough clearance for the precious metal, a trial run of a sheet of gilding-metal (G12–0.90 mm) should be pressed. It is an awkward process and the metal will need to be annealed at several stages before it will go into the mould properly, but after the first one has been done, following pressings in precious metal (which is more malleable) will be much easier, the impression in the die having been stretched and the lead compressed and hardened.

PART III: THE MECHANICAL PROCESSES

10   Spinning and turning

Spinning is a technique designed for producing in quantity rather than one single piece. It can also cut down the
hours of making something that would otherwise have to
be raised. If a simple straight-sided bowl is to be made, it
will be much quicker to turn the chuck (make a former)
and spin the bowl rather than to raise it, but if the bowl is
designed to neck in at any point, the piece need only be
spun up to that point, removed from the chuck and the
rest raised in. It will otherwise be impossible to remove
the chuck. In production workshops where a spinner is
employed to spin large quantities, he will make sectional
chucks over which the metal can be spun to any shape, the
chuck being made from sections that come to pieces and
so can be removed from the inside of the vessel. The
making of sectional chucks is highly skilled work and, if
pieces that need this technique are to be produced in
quantity, the job should be given to an out-worker. If
sectional chucks are not made properly, the marks left on
the metal by the separate sections would make more
work, the lines on the work would have to be knocked
out and the piece planished.

124 Spun silver and black enamel tea
set. Alex Telford, 1976

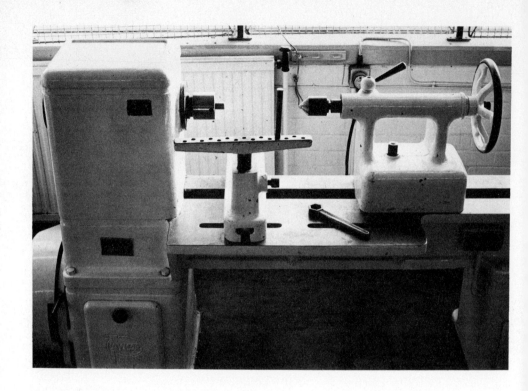

125 Spinning lathe

Spinning lathe

This is used to form metal over wooden or metal chucks or formers as well as for turning, and is operated on a simple system of belt and pulleys; when the switch on the machine is turned on the motor will start immediately. Most machines have two speeds. The wooden or metal chuck is screwed on to a 'false nose' attached to the nose on the spindle of the motor, and does not grasp the piece being worked as with the engineer's lathe, the metal is held in position against the face of the chuck by the follower, a small cylindrical piece of wood, which in turn is held in place by the tailstock. The tool-rest is a simple cast-iron slide to which is attached a t-bar with holes in its cross-bar into which a metal peg is slotted. The tool used is hand-held and cannot be attached to the tool-rest in any way. The position of the cast-iron slide can be altered as can the tool-rest, which can also be moved vertically.

Engineer's lathe

This is used for turning (cutting) metal, wood, ivory, etc. It has a metal chuck to hold the piece being turned, which may have three jaws that move together rather like a pin vice, or four jaws that move independently of each other. The tool is clamped into a tool-rest which holds it in a fixed position. The position of the tool-rest can be

altered, and there are two handles which move it along or
across the bed of the lathe. It may also have an automatic
threading device for cutting threads for screws. The
motor is operated through a system of gears, a switch
being pressed to turn it on and a gear-lever pulled to start
it.

126 Engineer's lathe

Both types of lathe have a headstock, made up of the
motor, spindle and chuck on the left-hand side of the
machine and a tailstock on the right, which can be
brought up to the chuck on the headstock and has several
functions. It is made of cast iron and has a wheel at one
end attached to a spindle called a 'quill' which moves in or
out when the wheel is turned. Slotted into it, by means of
a morse taper, is either a 'dead' or a 'live' centre; a short
steel bar with a point at one end which, when slotted in
the quill, lies directly in line with the centre point of the
chuck. The dead centre is fixed, moving only with the
quill; the live centre revolves on ball-bearings as well as
moving with the quill. The tailstock is used to steady
parts that stick out at some distance from the chuck to
hold the metal blank used for spinning in position, or the
centre can be removed and a drill-chuck attachment
inserted so that drilling can be done on the lathe. This can
be invaluable for drilling a hole in solid metal rod or
widening a hole in chenier.

A spinning lathe is far more robust than an engineer's
lathe. The pressure put on the machine when spinning

would eventually wear the bearings on an engineer's lathe, although a heavy duty wood-turning lathe could be used.

TOOLS AND MATERIALS

Wood (for chucks) If the chucks are made of wood it must be hardwood; beech is suitable for very small quantities but more often lignum vitae or boxwood are used. These can be used to turn out a larger quantity of work. Lignum tends to splinter and give off a resin that can jam the work on the chuck. Beech, boxwood or lignum vitae can be bought in cylindrical form as ready-made chucks but if a square block of wood is used then it must be cut to shape before being put on the lathe. The wood should be of a greater diameter than the widest part of the job, the length being at least 5 cm longer than the height of the job. The corners are cut off the block until it becomes a faceted circle, the centre point is found with a pair of dividers, and a small hole drilled. The wooden chuck will be screwed to the false nose on the lathe and so the hole must be opened out with a larger drill of the correct size to take the tap that corresponds with the screw on the false nose. The wood is then fixed into a vice and tapped (the size of the screw will be about 2.5 cm in diameter) and the chuck is screwed on to the lathe ready for turning.

If pieces are to be produced singly or in very small quantities, then it is cheaper and quicker to turn a wooden chuck. But there are advantages in using a metal chuck, apart from the fact that it does not wear so quickly: it is harder than a wooden one and so the blank can be stretched to a greater extent, metal can be moved around more, thickened in parts only and given a thick edge.

Metal (for chucks) Round section aluminium or brass is used; it must also be tapped to fit the lathe. If a piece is to be made in hundreds, then a brass chuck is turned; if in thousands, a steel chuck (brass tends to wear easily on detail). If an aluminium chuck is turned, it must be kept well greased or it may drag on the precious metal and cause scars. A slightly different turning tool is used with a rake back to stop the aluminium dragging when it is being turned to shape. Brass is much easier to turn than aluminium.

Metal (for spinning) Standard silver can be used although bullion dealers produce a special spinning alloy that is easier to handle. It is more malleable and will not bounce or spring as much as standard silver. Unless the metal is extremely hard when it is bought, it is not annealed until it has been drafted to a simple form on a wooden chuck. Britannia silver spins well.

Forming tools   These resemble over-sized burnishers and are approximately 60 cm long, of which a half is the wooden handle. There are several different shaped tools that can be used depending on the job being spun, but most forming and planishing is done with the same forming tool having two faces, one rounded for forming, the other flat for burnishing. Tools vary, some being more rounded than others; the more curved the face of the tool the more it will stretch the metal. A professional spinner will have several of these tools, one of which may have two rounded faces with different curves used for forming only. All spinning tools have softened edges, as sharp edges would dig into the metal, scratching or denting it.

Ball-ended tool   Has a slightly flattened ball-end and is used for sinking.

Ball-race   At the end of the tool, it is used for turning metal over, doubling it up, a technique used in spinning to give the impression of a thick edge. Because the ball-race runs along the metal rather than straight on to it, the metal does not become hot and work-hardened, and thus does not crack or need annealing.

Knurling tool   Has a hollowed wheel at its tip into which is fitted a tool that will reproduce a design that has been

127 Assorted chucks

139

128 Spinning-forming tools

cut into its surface. This process is normally done by a die-sinker.

Spade end   A flat tool, again with two faces, that splays out at the end. The top edge is flat and rounded: it is used for planishing flat pieces such as plates and trays.

Turning tools

Wood   An old file can be used as a wood-turning tool, the end being ground off to the correct angle, the face undercut about 45°. It is usually curved slightly across the top and undercut so that only the top edge is the cutting surface. Small files can be ground off to the corresponding curve for fitting into tight curves. The cutting face should always be slightly curved; a flat face can cause the tool to judder.

Metal   A piece of steel piping (8 mm diameter), 45 cm long, can be used as a tool-holder. A hole is drilled approximately 2.5 cm from the end to hold an Allan screw with which to lock the tool in position. The tool is made from 6 mm square section steel about 8 cm long, similar to that used on an engineer's lathe. For silver and brass the angle is ground off straight from the front edge of the tool; for aluminium it is given a rake back.

Turning tools are kept sharp on a grindstone, the edge of the tool being held up at the correct angle, approximately 45° from the front edge, supported where possible on the ledge in front of the wheel. When the tool begins to get hot it should be quenched before further grinding continues. It should be held firmly at the correct angle, one angle only being cut, so that when viewed from the front the tool should not have a series of facets. The grinding of tools should be practised, for it is important that they are kept sharp.

Arm-rest This is a square section piece of steel with a handle, the whole tool measuring 45 cm. The steel is hammered out and turned up at one end to form a short hook, used to support the turning tool when turning the face of a chuck, enabling it to be done without having to alter the tool-rest and reposition the cross-slide that supports it. The arm-rest is held in the left hand, supported on the tool-rest, the turning tool being held across it in the right hand.

129 Wood-turning tools

130 Metal-turning tools. *Left to right:* 1 tool with rake back, good for turning aluminium, 2 and 3 plain turning tools, 4 round-nosed turning tool, 5 parting off tool

131 Turning a wooden chuck

Turning the chuck

A template is made in aluminium, half the profile of the required chuck. It should be remembered that the thickness of the metal to be spun must be taken into consideration when taking the template from a drawing of the finished piece, the chuck being the *inside* dimension of the piece.

The facets on the sides of the chuck are turned away before it is shaped. The tool-rest is positioned parallel to the chuck, about 2.5 cm away from it, and the handle of the tool is held firmly in the right hand, itself supported by the tool-rest. The left hand supports the tool which is laid across the palm between the thumb and fingers, which hold the sides of the tool. When the face of the chuck needs to be turned, the arm-rest is used as described above.

The largest dimensions of the width and length of the piece are taken with a pair of outside callipers. The chuck is turned down to these dimensions, the callipers being help up to it at intervals to check the progress of the work. Once these parts have been turned to size, the rest of the chuck is formed by turning and holding the template to it until the correct shape is achieved. If it is a wooden chuck, the surface is finally smoothed with a worn hacksaw blade and sandpaper; if metal, with emery cloth. The surface of the chuck will transfer on to the inside of the metal form and so must be as smooth and polished as possible.

Spinning

Unless the finished piece is to be simple and shallow, the first stage of spinning is done on a wooden drafting-chuck, which is turned to a gentle sloping form, leaving less space between the precious metal and the chuck when it is transferred to the final chuck. If a deep form is being spun several drafting-chucks may be used to bring the form up slowly.

A blank can be calculated in the same way as for raising. The metal circle is held between the chuck and a follower, a small cylindrical piece of wood, which should always be as large as possible but slightly smaller than the base of the chuck. If a rounded form is being spun, the follower used should be slightly hollow. The tailstock is brought up so that the live centre holds the follower and metal blank in position, the blank being positioned as near the centre as possible. The tailstock is loosened very slightly, but it should still hold the metal in position, and the lathe is turned on: if it has two speeds, the slowest should be used. A flat piece of hardwood is held in the left hand, resting on the tool-rest, the top edge against the edge of the metal blank, centering it properly. The right

132–35 Spinning

hand must be placed on the wheel of the tailstock ready to tighten it when the metal runs true. Always stand to the right of the chuck at this point as the metal could fly off causing an accident. Loose clothing and jewellery should never be worn, and hair should always be tied back when operating a lathe. A professional spinner will turn on the machine before putting the metal against the chuck, centering it while the chuck is spinning, but this is inadvisable until considerable experience has been gained.

The tool-rest is now positioned, and should stand below the centre of the chuck (the actual height depending on the width of the chuck) and the distance from the chuck should be large enough just to clear the metal blank when it is in position. A peg should be slotted into the tool-rest slightly to the right of the edge of the disc, and the tool held with one end of the handle tucked under the right arm and the right hand around it. One should stand with one's feet slightly apart so that when spinning weight can be put firmly behind the tool without risk of falling over. The left hand should be placed at the junction of the handle with the tool, or round the peg.

The blank is now greased at intervals while forming the metal and is done to prevent the tool binding on and marking it. The grease used is beef tallow, spinner's soap or a hard-cup grease. It is applied by means of a cloth with its edges turned inwards, rolled into a bundle and tied, to prevent any loose ends catching on the lathe and pulling an operator's hands into the machine.

The rounded face of the tool is used against the sheet of metal below the horizontal centre of the chuck and as near the follower as possible. The tool, levered between the peg (on the right) and the metal (on the left), acts as a fulcrum and, as it is moved further up the chuck thus pushing the metal down, the peg is moved correspondingly up the holes on the tool-rest. With the pressure of the body behind it the tool is moved back and forth over the metal. The spinning should be done in as few strokes as possible, but the metal must sit down firmly on to the chuck. The distance covered with each stroke is short; occasionally a stroke is swept out to the edge of the metal, drawing it down, to make the metal at the base easier to draw in. Before any real shaping is done to the rest of the blank, the base must be drawn in completely yet the blank must be drawn in as a whole at the same time. As the metal is spun down on to the chuck, the tool is moved up a section and then that part is spun down.

Buckling of the outer edge of the blank during the first stages of spinning can be prevented by holding the flat wooden stick in the left hand behind the edge of the metal. If it should still buckle, the metal should be removed from the lathe, annealed and malleted flat on to a stake before being replaced on the lathe. The metal will harden while being worked, when it should be removed

136 Spun silver box with yew wood. Lindsey Middleton, 1970

and annealed. If the piece being spun has a narrow base, this may crack around the base line and need to be resoldered, even if, at a later stage, it is to be removed. If the base is to be rounded, the follower should be removed and the tailstock moved back when the sides of the piece have been spun. The base can then be spun down and planished, the left hand held over the piece to prevent it flying off the lathe, although the fact that the sides have been spun down will probably keep it in place.

Once the spinning has been completed the tool is turned over to its flat face and the metal planished as in spinning, that is by running the tool back and forth over the metal, burnishing out any spinning marks. Before the top edge of the metal is laid down flat on to the chuck it is turned true.

If a piece of work has to be spun to a certain weight and size, and it is stretching too much, it should be transferred to a smaller chuck with a step cut into it at the required height. The top edge is immediately spun into the step, and the rest of the metal is 'rolled in' or spun down, compressing it. A very slightly rounded spinning tool is used as the metal does not need to be stretched. The

137 Spun silver sphere box. Karina Payne, 1976

145

method is similar to that of back-raising, the metal being compressed and thickened, and can only be done on a metal chuck.

A thick edge can be created by spinning a small heavy gauge blank, such as G14 (1.10 mm) and stretching the metal, again on a metal chuck, but with a more rounded tool. The stretching is done at the base of the chuck, the top being stretched and worked as little as possible. When the metal is finally laid down on to the chuck, the face of the top edge is burnished with the flat side of the spinning tool to thicken it.

A vessel made from a thin gauge may need to be fortified in parts, such as a coffee-pot that needs strengthening at the junction of the body with the handle and spout. The metal can be 'packed in' by spinning down the top edge of the blank only, on a drafting chuck. The metal is transferred to another chuck to curve it slightly, not touching the angle on the top edge, and is finally transferred to the chuck of the required form. The curved top edge of the metal is laid down first, then the rest of the metal, to compress it. It can be thickened in different parts.

Spinning on air

A vessel that 'necks in' can be spun down on air as long as little detail is needed and the piece is not produced in quantity. The blank is spun to the point where it necks in, removed from the chuck and transferred to another of a diameter smaller than that of the part that is to be brought in, giving only a little support to the metal. The tailstock and follower are put in position giving some support to the metal, and it is carefully pushed down on air.

138 Spun silver coffee-pot. Robert Glover, 1977

139 Turning the top edge of a bowl

Turning

The tool-rest is moved close to the chuck and the tool laid across it, firmly held in both hands. If the rest is too far away, the edge of the tool may catch in the metal and not be supported well enough to stop it jamming in the lathe. The metal will chip at first, as only the high spots are being cut away, but this will turn into a streamer of metal as the top begins to turn true.

An open-ended cylinder is formed from a flat circle in the normal way, and the base line is turned, allowing the bottom to fall out, pushing back the tailstock and removing the follower once the cylinder has been spun, re-positioning the tool-rest to turn the base line.

If a strengthening wire, such as may be used on a napkin-ring, is to be turned to relieve it of some weight, a wooden chuck is turned with a slight taper to fit the inside diameter of the ring. The napkin-ring is pushed on to the chuck with a wooden stick and will expand slightly with friction, moving further up the chuck. When it is firmly in place it should be cooled with a rag which will shrink it on to the chuck. The rag should be folded in the same way as the one used to apply grease. Once the turning has been done the stick is levered between the peg and the back edge of the napkin-ring to remove it from the chuck.

The base ring and the top edge of a beaker can be turned by turning a chuck to fit the inside of the vessel. The chuck does not have to be the same shape as the vessel but it must fit tightly inside a section of it, not the top edge.

Turning on an engineer's lathe is far more precise than a spinning lathe. The tool is held in a cross slide and can be repositioned and moved forwards and inwards by turning the handle at the end and side of the lathe. Unfortunately not all pieces of work can be fitted satisfactorily on to an engineer's lathe, but it can be used for turning rod, tubing, wire, etc.

140 Spun silver pepper mill with ebony top. Anthony Elson, 1978

141 Spun silver goblets. Top and base of stem spun, rubber mould taken and then cast for reproduction. Frances Loyen, 1979

142 Paper-weight, bell, candle-snuffer, paper-knife and spoons, showing use of casting, spinning and forging. Brian Fuller, 1979

11   Casting

Casting is a way of producing a form by pouring metal into a mould of the required shape, the mould having been previously formed round an original pattern. Three-dimensional forms that would otherwise be carved from a solid piece of metal can be made this way. The pattern can be made in wax, wood, steel or resin among other materials. Reproductions are cast, from the pattern which should be made with precision, having a surface as accurate as possible. As the metal will shrink when cast, the pattern should be made slightly larger than actually required.

The same technique can be used to reproduce a piece in twos or threes, or in thousands. In jewellery-making it is used for complete pieces like rings and brooches. With silversmithing, although whole pieces can be made by casting, more often separate parts are cast, and soldered or riveted on to a larger piece. Stems for goblets, sockets for coffee-pot handles or simply decorated pieces are made this way.

Several methods of casting are used by silversmiths: investment, sand and cuttlefish. The one used depends on the nature of the work, and must be considered before the job is done, preferably at the design stage. Casting equipment is expensive and highly technical to use so that it is generally found to be more economical to send work out to a specialist firm than to do it in a small studio.

Investment casting

This technique normally used for small to medium-sized objects, the pattern being made from wax or other material that can be burnt out of the mould without leaving any residue, and is employed a great deal in jewellery-making. The various flasks that can be bought in to which to pour the mould are large enough to hold such patterns, making this an inexpensive way of producing small articles, but for the considerably larger pieces that a silversmith might want to have cast it is more costly than sand-casting. It does, however, produce

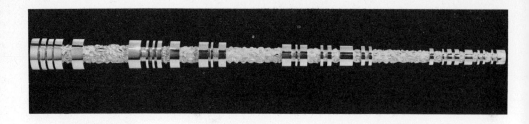

143 Silver mace. Cast in separate parts
and then soldered together. 1.52 m
long. Jocelyn Burton, 1977

144 Silver butter dish with applied
castings. Jocelyn Burton, 1979

145 Detail of above

146 Two candle-holders with cast
decoration, one squat, one vase-shaped
Brian Asquith, 1975

pieces with a finish superior to the other types of casting and is used in silversmithing when small castings are required.

Investment is a fast-setting mixture of plaster and silica in the form of quartz and cristobalite. It is capable of withstanding great heat without cracking (see p. 164). It is poured over a wax pattern (or other material such as wood and paper, etc.) and allowed to dry. The pattern is then melted or burned out and replaced by molten metal. Once this has been done, the mould is destroyed to remove the cast piece. If more than one piece is required an original pattern is made in metal and a rubber die is formed around it. This die is then cut open, the pattern removed, the die closed and wax injected into it. The metal pattern is made up in a metal that cannot be harmed by the heat of the machine used to make the rubber die. It is formed or carved and polished to the desired finish. It can be polished and then rhodium-plated in order to protect it against the rubber vulcanizing agent (see below) which will attack the surface of alloys containing copper, silver or nickel, causing a roughness that is reproduced in the rubber die. The die is extremely flexible and the pattern can easily be removed from it, however many undercuts it may have, so that this type of casting has an advantage over other methods.

147 Figures modelled in wax and cast in silver (investment casting). Mary Dean, 1978

Making a sprue

The sprue is a passage through which molten metal is poured; it must be attached to a suitable part of the pattern. It is necessary not only to enable the molten metal to flow easily into the mould, but also for the melted wax to run into the rubber die. The most suitable shape for the sprue is round in cross-section, and this should be at least equal in size to the biggest cross-section of the pattern. The sprue should also be arranged so that the molten metal can flow easily into all parts of the cavity, and it should lead to the heaviest part of the pattern. The sprue should not have a sharp edge where it

148 Wax replica of metal pattern

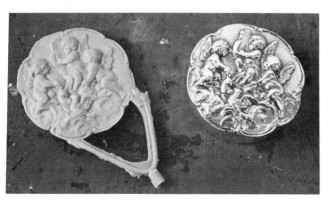

joins the pattern. The sprue is attached to the model before the rubber die is made; it should not be attached to heavily decorated areas if possible, as it will finally be cut off, leaving a flat area that would have to be decorated; nor should it be attached to thin stalks that open up into wide areas, as the metal will not flow through them easily. Incorrect sprueing can result in incomplete castings, porosity and surface shrinkage. If a pattern is large and heavy or particularly intricate and delicate, two sprues should be attached, giving the metal easier access to the pattern.

They can be bought ready-made in wax, but it is better to form them in the rubber die by taking a piece of round-section metal wire and soldering another larger piece to one end of it, the narrower end being soldered carefully to the metal pattern.

The rubber die

The die is made of several sheets of unvulcanized rubber, the amount depending on the size of the pattern. Each one should be approximately 3 mm thick, and they are vulcanized round a pattern to form a solid elastic block. Vulcanizing is the treatment of rubber with sulphur at a high temperature in order to increase its elasticity, strength and yield. the block is formed in an aluminium frame and the sheets of rubber are cut to fit into this. The pattern must fit easily into the frame, leaving a border about 2.5 cm between it and the frame. This is in order to prevent distortion of the die around the pattern which may happen if it lies too near the frame. The sheets of rubber are cut with scissors and then laid in the frame. The pattern is put in position when the frame is half full. If any parts of the metal protrude, giving large undercuts,

149 Sheet rubber being placed in an aluminium frame

150 Vulcanizing press

small snippets of rubber should be packed around them. The rubber sheets that lie next to the pattern should be absolutely grease-free, and wiped over with Genklene to remove any grease or dirt on their surfaces. The frame is fitted to the top with rubber sheets and the outside of the mould is dusted with chalk. The frame that holds the rubber die is made up of two parts that locate together. At one end is a round hold (a half-round section on each side of the frame) through which the sprue will project, giving a straight path to the pattern. This also acts as a guide to opening the rubber die.

When the rubber has been packed into the frame, it is placed in a vulcanizing press, between two thermostatically controlled, electrically heated platterns. The press is screwed down as the rubber begins to soften and spread over the top of the mould frame, but it should not be tightened down on to the aluminium frame too hard or the pressure will break it.

Vulcanizing will take from thirty minutes upwards, depending on the thickness of the die.

 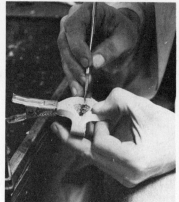 

Cutting the die

The solid block is cut to release the pattern. Registration locks must be cut to enable the two halves to be fitted together exactly. The sprue protruding from one end of the die will act as a guide-line for cutting the die. A line is cut around the outside of the die with a sharp scalpel, about 1.5 mm deep, and the registration locks are formed by cutting into one side of the rubber, along and down again. As the rubber is cut it is gently pulled apart. All but the most complex patterns can be made in a two-part die.

Waxes

There are many different types of wax that can be used for making patterns for investment casting. Commercially made waxes, jewellery and dental waxes may be bought in many forms: some are better for carving, being hard and slightly brittle; others are more plastic, while some are soft enough to be modelled with the fingers. They are sold in block, sheet, wire and tube form. Waxes can be made up or blended in the workshop using vegetable waxes such as carnauba and candelilla wax, mineral waxes such as ceresine, as well as the more commonly known beeswax. Since the large range of commercially produced waxes is adequate for every need, however, it is unnecessary to make them up in the workshop.

The modelling is done either by carving the wax after warming it, so that it can be worked with modelling tools or with the fingers (it is often easier to mount the wax on dowelling first), or by heating the tool in a flame and using this to melt and model the wax. The tools used can be made from steel or wood. Dentists will often give away worn instruments which can be made into the required shape by forging or filing the ends.

If the tool is heated on a flame a bunsen burner or a methylated spirits burner should be used; a candle flame

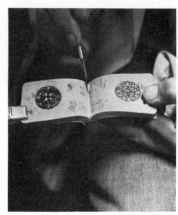

will give off soot that will form particles of grit in the casting flask and so damage the casting.

The pattern can also be made from a natural object such as a leaf, an insect or a piece of paper, provided it can be burnt out completely. If this is likely to be distorted or destroyed when the plaster is poured on to it, it should be lightly dipped in varnish to protect its shape.

Wax injection

Wax is injected into the rubber die to reproduce the pattern. Many waxes are available commercially, combining high fluidity and low shrinkage, that are tough and elastic. The cavity of the die is brushed lightly with talc to prevent the wax from sticking to it, and any excess must be blown or brushed away. The talc should be brushed into the cavity only, or the wax will flow into the rest of the die, leaving a line or a thin 'fin' of wax where the two halves join. Any excess should be carefully removed with a cloth.

151–57 Cutting open a rubber die

The wax injector will heat the wax, the two halves of the rubber die are then held together and the molten wax is injected through the sprue hole. The temperature of the wax should be about 60° C; if it is hotter it will stick to the rubber; if it is cooler, it will not run freely into the die. The exact temperature will depend on the type of wax used. The cavity may have to be brushed with talc after every three or four waxes have been taken, again depending on the type of wax used. The die should be left to cool at intervals.

Setting up the wax model

Before the waxes are set up in the casting flask they must be weighed to see how much metal is needed to cast them. The wax can be assumed to have a specific gravity

158 Setting up a wax model

159 Tree of cast pieces

of 1. Thus the weight of the metal required is the weight of wax multiplied by the specific gravity of the metal to be used. In the case of standard silver, this factor is 10. The weight of the wax for the sprue should be added and also a button of wax at the end of the sprue.

The sprue is set up on the wax button (about 1.2 mm in diameter) which sits on a mound in the centre of the rubber base. If a flat sheet of rubber is used for the base, the mound should be built up with wax. The wax button will leave a large opening when it is burned out to enable the metal to run into the mould easily. The sprue is attached by warming a metal tool and running it between both pieces of wax to be joined. If only one piece of wax is melted the joint will not be secure and may part when the investment is poured into the flask. If several waxes are mounted in one flask to form a tree, the centre sprue, to which each pattern and its sprue is attached, must be wide enough to carry enough metal to replace the waxes which are removed, and allow for shrinkage. The waxes should be no closer than 1 mm to each other, and should be set up in such a way as to ensure that as little air as possible can be trapped in or behind them. If a wax is set up that takes the form of a hollow object with a small opening and the investment, inside the hollow, has only a small connec-

160 Cast cup in silver and bronze.
Robert Marsden, 1976

tion leading to the bulk of the investment, silver wires are
sunk into the wax before investing it. Thus, when the
wax is melted out, the inner core of investment is supported by the wires, and when the piece is cast the wires
are soldered in position on the cast piece to secure them. If
a flat sheet of rubber is used with a wax mound and
several pieces are to be cast in one flask the sprues can be
attached straight to the wax base mound.

The flask size should be chosen to allow at least 3 mm
between the patterns and side of the flask, and 12 mm at
the top. It is slipped over the waxes and set on the rubber
base, a thin layer of wax being melted around the junction
of the two to prevent the investment running out when
the flask is being filled. If the waxes have a coating of talc
on them, they should be dipped in a solution of detergent
and water which is then washed off completely. Excess
detergent on the pattern will cause foaming in the
investment, leading to nodules on the cast pieces.

The investment

This should be mixed in a rubber or plastic bowl (a
flexible bowl makes it easier to remove excess). Care
should be taken to avoid mixing air with it. This has to be

157

161 Vacuum chamber and flasks

removed before the mixture sets (see *Vacuum chamber* below).

The manufacturer's instructions should be carefully followed, the powder weighed, water measured and used at a known temperature to obtain consistent results. The investment is thoroughly mixed to form a thick creamy paste that will pour easily into the mould. A defoaming agent may be mixed with the water before adding the investment to help release the air bubbles. If too much water is used the investment will dry away from the wax leaving it indistinct or porous; if it is too thick it may set before the flask is filled, trapping air bubbles and not coating the model properly. The investment should not be poured into the flask immediately (see manufacturer's instructions). When ready it should be poured slowly into the flask, filling it evenly rather than being splashed in to ensure proper coating.

Vacuum chamber

When the flask is full the air is taken out by putting it into a small chamber with a pressure gauge which, by vacuum, will remove all the air bubbles in the flask. A piece of paper can be wrapped around the top of the flask to form a collar to contain the investment when the air is being removed. The mixture will bubble and the chamber should be rocked, jiggling the flask and helping the investment to settle around the wax pattern. The flask is removed from the chamber and the investment allowed to set before the paper collar is removed, the top of the investment levelled and excess cleaned from the sides of the flask.

Investing without a vacuum chamber

Another method of investing a wax, if a vacuum chamber is not available, is to set up the wax on the rubber base and

162 Burn-out furnace and crucible

paint it with the investment, making sure that no air bubbles are trapped. When it is set but still wet, the flask is put in position around it and filled with investment. This is allowed to dry until no external moisture is apparent. The time will depend on the size of the flask, and varies from one to four hours. The rubber base is then removed.

Burn-out furnace

The flask is put into an oven to burn out the wax. Unless the burn-out furnace is specially made to give a pre-burn-out, the initial de-waxing should be done either in a lower temperature oven, or a converted wash-boiler, that will steam the wax out. The flask is placed on a shelf in the oven with a saucer under it to collect the wax. Once it has been burnt out, the sprue opening will show a layer of carbon (black) which has not burnt off. At this point the flask is transferred to the burn-out furnace.

The flask is placed, again sprue opening downwards, in the furnace, which is then turned on. It is heated slowly to 300° C, being brought to 200° C in the first hour, and the temperature increased and maintained in the second. It is then taken up to 700–50° C. The time taken to burn out the residue of wax depends on the size of the flask. It may take two hours, or six, or longer. There must be an adequate flow of air through the furnace for the carbon to burn out completely: it will be seen to have been burnt out when the sprue hole glows red. The flask is then ready for casting. The whole process of burning out the wax is done slowly to prevent the investment from cracking. It must be dried out completely, however, or steam will form in the mould, either destroying it or causing bad castings.

The temperature of the flask must be brought down for the casting process: how much depends on the section of the patterns used. It should be as low as possible, but if

163 Centrifugal casting machine.
Melting the metal

it is too low, the investment is liable to crack when the metal is poured on it, or it could hinder the flow of the metal, causing it to solidify before it has filled the cavity. If the temperature is too high it may cause shrinkage, porosity and coarse grain structure in the cast metal. For silver it should be between 350°C and 650°C.

Machinery used for investment casting

There are various types of machines used, whether the chosen system is centrifugal or vacuum-assisted. A centrifugal machine is made up of two arms revolving on a support, one arm holding the crucible for melting the metal with the flask holding the mould, the other the weights that counter-balance the arm. These weights can be adjusted according to the size of the flask used. The machine is operated by a spring which, when released, sends the arms spinning round, throwing the molten metal from the crucible into the flask. The arm may operate on either a horizontal or a vertical plane. There is a 'splatter' shield around the arm to protect the user from any molten metal that may spray off when the machine is in use, which can happen if too much metal has been melted. The metal is melted in the crucible on the centrifugal machine only when the flask has cooled to the right temperature, which is seen when the sprue hole is dark red. The flask is put in place and the metal is melted in the crucible which is in line with the flask, a hole at one end of the crucible leading directly into the sprue hole of the mould.

A vacuum-assisted casting machine can also be used. It is made up of a vacuum chamber with a casting head attached, but instead of the metal being thrown into the mould, as with the centrifugal casting machine, it is forced in by atmospheric pressure. For large casting the metal is melted in a crucible in a furnace and poured into the mould; for smaller ones it is melted directly in the mould. A simple hand vacuum-assisted casting machine can also be used. The flask is attached to the casting head on the machine and it is turned on as the molten metal is poured into the mould. Because of the porosity of the investment a vacuum is formed in the mould and the metal is pushed into it by the atmospheric pressure surrounding it.

Melting the metal

The metal used must be as clean as possible, solder and any base metal or impurities that go into the melt will not only give a bad, porous casting, but may also bring down the standard of the metal, making it impossible to hallmark. Lemel should not be used as it contains too many impurities. Snippets of clean scrap metal are preferable. Casting grain can be bought from a bullion dealer.

Melting the precious metal must be done carefully; a pinch of borax or lump charcoal is added to the metal as it begins to melt to protect it from oxides which will cause bad colour, a poor finish and probable loss of ductility. As it starts to melt the metal will form a bead and begin to spin, and at this point the casting process commences.

If the metal is cast in a crucible (there are many sizes) that can be attached to the centrifugal machine, the casting is done in one action when the arm is released. If it is a large casting, as used in a vacuum-assisted casting machine, it is melted in a furnace and tipped into the mould. Again charcoal should be added to the melt to keep it protected from oxides. The crucible in which it has been melted should be held as short a distance as possible from the top of the mould and the metal poured in carefully, any slag being held back with a skimmer or a steel bar. When the flask has been cast and the colour of the investment at the sprue hole has faded from red, the flask can be quenched to remove the piece of work. The investment will disintegrate and the metal can be thoroughly cleaned by the use of sand-blasting, brushing, steam-cleaning or an ultrasonic cleaner.

Sand-casting

This is a form of casting used when pieces are needed in relatively small quantities or if they are too large to be cast in any other way. Several different sizes can be cast in one mould and other moulds are taken from that one. The patterns can be made in wood, plaster, resin, metal, or any material that will keep its shape when packed in sand.

It should not have undercuts as the process for making moulds for such pieces is extremely complicated and demands a high degree of skill. However, such pieces can be made in separate parts to be soldered together later.

As the sand used must bind well under pressure and, when cut, stay firm with clean-cut edges, it must not be too wet. A clay-bonded sand called 'marl' is therefore used. In a report published by the Technical Advisory Committee of the Worshipful Company of Goldsmiths (No. 4a/2) the following mixture of sands and binders is recommended:

75% Ryarsh sand
20% Mansfield sand
4%   Genuine Wyoming bentonite
1%   Kordek D 1205 (a cereal sand-binder)

for suppliers see Appendices

The two sands should be thoroughly mixed before the bentonite and Kordek are added. The moisture content should be adjusted to between 3 and 4 per cent. The preparing or 'tempering' of the sand is done by adding water to the pile and cutting it in. The sand is ready if it forms a solid ball when grasped in the hand. A minimum of water should be used.

Sand moulds for silver-casting are usually made in knob-hole boxes, which are made of cast iron and consist of two halves, the cope and the drag – the top and bottom of the box respectively. Both are open frames in which the sand is supported by mould boards that are clamped on to the top and bottom. The only difference between the cope and the drag is that the lower box, the drag, has pins that slot into holes in the cope locating them together in the middle.

The cope is laid down on a mould board with the locating holes uppermost. A layer of sand is sprinkled into it, pressed down firmly and slowly built up, the top layer being flattened with a mallet or a hammer. The

164 Knob-hole box

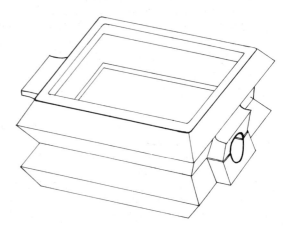

pattern is pushed firmly into the sand, up to its half-way point. If there is more detail on one side than the other, it should be left protruding from the sand. The first side into which the pattern is pushed, known as the 'odd side', provides only a temporary support for the pattern.

At one end of the cope there is a half-round hole that corresponds with a similar hole in the drag, forming what will become the round sprue hole. A piece of dowel or metal rod is placed in the hole leading to the pattern but not touching it. If several patterns are to be cast in the same box they should be arranged around the sprue, lying flat alongside it, so that they can easily be fed by it when the metal is poured in. The top surface of the sand is dusted with parting powder (burnt brick dust or bone ash).

The drag is now placed on top of the cope, the locating pins being seated in the appropriate holes. The knob-hole box is then filled with sand which is sprinkled evenly through a coarse sieve (a riddle) until the model is just covered. It is packed in tightly with the fingers and should be roughened slightly to help key the next layer of sand that is also pushed down firmly with the fingers and then malleted. If the box is still not full, the surface should be roughened, more sand being added until the box is full. It should again be malleted down firmly, levelled and a mould board put on top.

The odd side (cope) and the drag are turned over, and the odd side removed. The pattern should remain in the drag because the sand has been packed in so tightly around it. If it does not, it should be carefully lifted out of the odd side and put into the recess in the drag. Although two separate recesses have been made, forming the complete shape of the pattern, the half made in the odd side will not be as distinct as that made in the drag, so a complete casting cannot be made successfully from these two halves.

A cope is now slotted on top of the drag, and sand is packed firmly around the pattern until the cope is filled. A board is rested on top, cope and board are removed and further reproductions of the pattern are made by filling another cope.

Once the moulds have been made they are separated, the pattern and dowel for the sprue are removed and small channels (called 'gates') are cut with a scalpel leading from the sprue to the pattern. The positions of the gates must be carefully considered. If, for example, a model of an animal is to be cast, a gate should be cut running from one leg to the next. This is cut off when the casting is removed from the mould. The size of the gates depends on the section and size of the pattern: gates should always be cut leading out of the recess (not into it) and they must not lead to an intricate part of the pattern. Any sand that may fall into the recess should be carefully brushed or blown away, and any surface that has been cut should be gently painted with a sodium silicate solution, using a small brush: this will bind the newly cut sand. Vents are also cut leading from the mould cavity to the same end as the main pouring sprue, or to an edge, thus allowing gases and steam to escape. Without the vents the casting would be incomplete and the mould destroyed.

The mould is now dried. In industry it used to be the practice to dry the moulds in front of open coke braziers but they are now dried in an oven or, in a small work-shop, in front of a fire or next to the kiln.

When they are dry the two faces of the mould are given a coating of soot; this is a process known as 'torching' which helps the metal run easily into the mould. The faces of the mould are suspended over burning resin, an extremely dirty process. An alternative is to use a sooty flame on a gas torch, but resin is considered superior in helping the flow of silver. Torching is necessary for silver but not for gold, brass or bronze. With the recommended sand the skin-drying obtained during torching should be sufficient for moulds used for silver-casting.

The two sides of the moulds are now closed, opened and checked and any particles of sand brushed or blown away before clamping the mould together for casting.

The metal should be melted quickly and lump wood-charcoal is added to protect it from the air. Water should always be kept away from molten metal; it will spatter if it does have contact, and in a mould it will cause an explosion and destroy the casting. The crucible in which the metal is to be melted should be dry and as clean as possible. In foundries it is usual to add a piece of white cast iron or a bit of an old file to the melt in order to refine the grain structure of the metal and reduce the occurrence of 'hot tearing' (the tearing of the cast metal into irregular cracks with oxidized surfaces). The metal is melted, preferably in a furnace, although a gas-air torch can be used as an alternative. The molten metal is lifted as little a distance as possible directly above the mould with short tongs that clamp snugly around the crucible. There should be no delay between lifting the crucible and pour-ing. Slag is held back with a skimmer or an old file. The mould is tipped at a slight angle so that the metal runs down the mould surface and does not splash straight into the mould; pouring too slowly may make the metal solidify so that it does not fill the cavity completely. The mould is left to cool; the colour of the metal and the heat given off by the sprue is an indication as to whether or not the metal is cold.

Cuttlefish-casting

This is a simple and cheap form of casting. Cuttlefish can be bought from pet shops or ironmongers. The surface of the cast piece is not particularly good but if a simple form is to be cast, it can be filed easily or carved into a more intricate shape. Patterns with undercuts are too complicated to make in cuttlefish casting. They would have to be carved into the cuttlefish rather than being pressed into it in the normal way, and the cuttlefish would have to be broken to remove the precious metal.

The faces of two pieces of cuttlefish are filed flat with a hand file so that they fit together with no rocking or movement. The cuttlefish is soft enough to allow one to scrape it out with a fingernail, but it retains clear-cut edges if handled carefully. Two matchsticks, broken into four pieces (or four small ball-bearings) are pushed deep into one face, one at each corner. The other piece of cuttlefish is pushed against this, the matchsticks being pressed into position. The two sides are pulled apart and the pattern is pushed into one side, down to half of its height. It may have to be removed after the initial impression is made in order to scrape out some of the cuttlefish. When this half-impression has been made, the pattern is taken out and the cuttlefish dust removed. The pattern is replaced and the two sides are pushed together. The scraping-out process may have to be repeated on the other piece of cuttlefish so that the two faces fit together.

Once the complete recess is made the pattern is removed, the cuttlefish dust cleaned away and small air vents cut with a scalpel from various points around the pattern to the outside edge of the cuttlefish.

A sprue hole is cut to take the molten metal, tapered out at the end to facilitate pouring. The two halves are bound together with binding wire and the bottoms of the two sides of cuttlefish, which are pointed, are cut off to give a flat base. The mould is supported in a box of sand and the piece is ready to be cast, in the same manner as sand-casting.

Casting an ingot

If a piece of metal or wire is needed of a greater thickness than can be bought, it can be cast in two ways. For a large quantity and for long lengths the metal can be melted in a crucible (as for sand-casting) either in a furnace or with a blowtorch, and poured into a cast-iron ingot mould. A cast-iron block with channels is available in varying sizes. Alternatively one can scrape out the form in a charcoal block, and melt the metal in the cavity, first sprinkling the surface with borax.

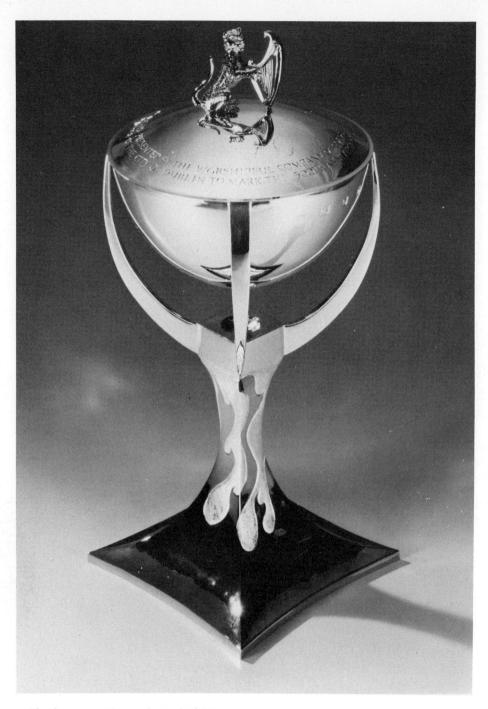

165 Silver loving cup with textured stem. Sarah Jones, 1978

PART IV: THE FINISHING PROCESSES

12 Polishing

Polishing is done by hand or machine using different grades of abrasives to produce the desired finish on a piece of work. There are two main stages: the first is to grind or sand away the surface of the metal, using abrasives, each of a finer grade than the last. This removes deep blemishes, but leaves a series of fine scratches on the surface of the metal. The second stage is to buff and shine the metal, using fine abrasives; the friction causes the surface of the metal to melt very slightly, so that it flows over the fine scratches. Each stage of finishing has an element of another in it. (The 'smeared' second stage of polishing is called the 'Beilby layer', named after Sir George Beilby who developed the process in 1921.)

The preparation for finishing a piece of work is done while the piece is being constructed. Making unnecessary marks on the surface of the metal should be avoided. When, for instance, a coffee-pot has to have a spout soldered on to it, all firestain and file-marks should be removed before it is assembled in order to retain clear-cut edges and a clean finish. If such an imperfect surface is polished *after* the coffee-pot has been assembled the edges will be softened and a less professional finish is achieved. Polishing is not a technique 'tacked on' to the end of a piece of work; it must be considered when the piece is being designed and during its construction. Although the problems of polishing should not constrain the design, they must be taken into consideration. If the design of a piece is such that the construction will make the polishing difficult, the required degree of finish will not be achieved. It may be preferable to construct a piece made up of intricate parts by using rivets or screws in order that the pieces can be polished first and then assembled.

Specialist polishers are employed by large-scale workshops because they work quickly as the result of continual practice and also because the technique requires a high degree of skill. There are different polishers for largework and smallwork since the problems involved are different.

Equipment

The two stages of polishing can both be carried out using a polishing motor, although the first stage is often done by hand. The polishing motor should run at a speed of 2800 rpm to be at its most efficient and must be bolted firmly to a bench or, if free-standing, to the floor. Great care should be taken, and, as always when machinery is in use, loose hair should be tied back. The job must never be held in a cloth, which will catch easily on the spindle causing an unpleasant accident. If work does get caught on the mop, let go at once. It is better to have to remake the job than to risk injury.

It is useful to have an extractor attached to the polishing motor as finishing is a dirty job. All the polish and dust should be collected together after polishing, for this can be sold to a bullion dealer who will recover the precious metal from it. The surface around the polishing motor, although dirty, must be kept clear of metal filings, emery dust and so on. A small grain caught on the mop will cause deep scratches that will take the polishing back to its early stages.

A burnisher, a polished steel, agate or haematite tool, is also required.

FIRST STAGE

SANDING AND GRINDING MATERIALS

Trent sand   Used mainly in largework, it is so abrasive that in unskilled hands it can ruin a piece of work and its proper use requires much practice. It consists of a fine sand mixed with vegetable oil and is used on a felt and leather bob. It can also be mixed with pumice powder and a small amount of oil is sufficient to make it bind when it is squeezed in the hand.

Pumice   Used for removing scratches and file marks. It comes in powder or rock form. The former is mixed with vegetable oil and applied to a felt bob, in the same manner as Trent sand – some polishers use it as an alternative. It comes in several grades and is used for polishing enamelled work. (G120 hole.) In rock form, pumice powder is used with water in the same manner as a hand file, being rubbed across the scratches; it leaves a coarse finish that can be removed with water of Ayr stone, emery paper or wet and dry paper.

Emery   A mixture of carborundum and magnetite or haematite, it is used mounted on cloth or paper to remove file marks. It can be bought in powder form and applied to the work on a felt bob, but it is extremely abrasive. Polishing papers can be fine enough to impart a reflective surface to the metal.

Emery composition   Comes in bar form and is a mixture of grease and emery powder. There are three grades, the medium grade only being used for precious metals. When the piece has been sanded, it is brushed with emery composition before being assembled.

Silicone carbide or carborundum   Mounted on waterproof paper, it can be used wet without the paper disintegrating (wet and dry paper). Harder than emery, it does not wear so quickly and comes in several grades. It is easier to handle than emery paper.

Water of Ayr stone   A natural soft slate used for removing scratches, file marks and firestain. It is used a great deal in polishing smallwork. It is bought in sticks ranging from 2 mm square to 2.5 cm square.

Wet and dry paper   See *Silicone carbide*.

Bobs   Various shaped felt bobs are used to apply Trent sand and pumice: they can be bought in different sizes and cut to shape, or the felt can be bought in a large block and cut up. Once the approximate shape has been cut with a knife, the sides and face can be shaped with a pumice stone or a hacksaw blade while the bob is running on the polishing motor. Leather bobs can be bought in different sizes, again for use with Trent sand and pumice, and they are used where a felt bob would wear down quickly, such as when a series of steps in a base wire is being polished. For this type of job the leather is cut back sharply from its face leaving a narrow ridge that will fit easily into the angle, since, if it were done with a felt, it would wear down quickly and round off the edges of the metal. Leather bobs are also more flexible than felt. The sizes can be from 1.5 cm (diameter) upwards and there are many different widths.

   Once the piece has been made it is sent to the assay office in its rough state before being polished and when it has been returned the marks on its surface caused by scraping are cleaned off with a file. File marks and any pitt marks on the metal are then removed by grinding or sanding the surface.

GRINDING (STONING OR SANDING)

By hand   Stoning is usually done on smallwork where a true flat surface is required. A water of Ayr stone is dipped in water and used in the same way as a hand file. If the scratches are deep, a pumice stone is used before the

166 Stoning

water of Ayr but care should be taken as the stones often contain impurities which can cause even heavier scratches.

The stoning process takes a long time, scratches and firestain being removed, but if done properly the resulting surface is really smooth and even. A file is used on flat boxes across their surfaces to remove all firestain and marks, and to ensure that they are perfectly flat. Any distortions in the surface, although seemingly very slight at this stage, will show up at the final polishing, making the work look very shoddy. It is then stoned across the file marks until an even white sheen is achieved.

When a piece of largework has been assembled, there may be small areas that need stoning that cannot be reached by a bob on the polishing motor which may also soften off the corners of an adjacent wire.

If the box is small enough, the flat sides can be rubbed wet on to wet and dry paper firmly attached to a surface plate. This must be held down on all sides or it will curl up and round off the corners and sides of the box. Emery and wet and dry papers can be used wrapped around a file or a stick of wood of appropriate section. Fine polishing papers are used in this way until all the marks left by the water of Ayr stone are removed.

Less filing is done on largework and most of it is done to remove marks on the surface. These are removed by wet and dry paper on a file, covering a larger surface of metal than is necessary. If two parts of a piece have been polished and assembled by soldering, and there is an excess of solder around the joint this is removed with a fine file, the file marks being removed with wet and dry paper or water of Ayr stone.

By machine The polishing motor is used by attaching bobs, brushes or mops to it by means of a tapered thread. The wheel must always turn towards the polisher. The metal is applied to the mop below the centre of the wheel so that it is not thrown off; it is polished from the centre outwards, towards the edges of the metal. The edges are never put straight up against the wheel or they will catch and the metal will be thrown off. Protruding pieces should be applied straight to the mop rather than led in from another part of the job; this would cause the edges to round off and probably catch on the wheel.

The grinding and polishing actions should always follow the form of the work. Wires are polished with felts or leather bobs where possible to retain their flatness; curved forms are followed through, rather than being polished in a series of strokes that will leave flats on the surface of the metal.

If Trent sand or pumice powder is used, it is fed on to the top side of the bob, being pulled down between the bob and the felt. It is kept in a tray beneath the spindle, and is fed in when the bob begins to run dry. The sanding process depends on an even flow of sand running between the felt and the metal. It should be used with the greatest care and only after the technique has been practised. It will remove spinning and stamping marks as well as file marks and firestain. Several felt bobs, each a different shape and size, are used to fit various parts of a job, the curves and right angles. If a wrongly shaped felt is used, then the corners will be rubbed off and the contours distorted. The sanding will leave a dull white satin finish which will show up any deep pitted marks on the surface of the metal or pin-holes in the solder. These marks should be sanded or filed over a larger area than they take up or a dip will show where they have been gouged out. Large pin-holes would have been noticed earlier and plugged with wire.

Pressure is put on the mop and the sanding is done *across* the scratch lines; if it is done along them the resulting drag lines would be camouflaged by the sanding lines and not show until a later polishing stage. The job is kept moving continually to spread the heat and to prevent the metal from being sanded unevenly. A piece of work that is badly sanded will have its form changed completely.

Once the work has been sanded, it is cleaned thoroughly with detergent and a soft brush, and then brushed on the machine with an emery composition. The work is usually sanded before it is assembled, and brushing with the emery composition after assembling will remove any firestain that is near the surface. Care should be taken to solder the work as quickly and cleanly as possible. The greater number of times that a piece of work is heated, the deeper will be the firestain, making it harder to remove.

If flat sheets of metal, such as picture frames or plaques to be engraved, are to be polished on the machine they are held against a piece of wood with nails at each corner securing them in position to prevent the edges of the metal from being rounded off.

167 Brushing

Firestain

There are different ways of approaching this problem. It can be prevented to some extent by the use of an anti-firestain solution (see p. 82), although this tends just to prevent it from penetrating too deeply under the surface. When a piece has been finished, the firestain will not have formed an even covering on the metal, but will be patchy. It can be removed by sanding, stoning and polishing, or covered by polishing the metal to a good finish, ignoring the patches of fire, and then silver-plating the piece. But this latter method is not permanent and the plate will wear in patches showing the firestain beneath it. The final method is to polish the metal to a good finish, then heat it, let it cool and pickle it, repeating this several times until the layer of firestain is even all over. The metal is then given a final rouge polish, which gives it an even bluish grey colour.

SECOND STAGE

Once the piece has been stoned it is polished. All grit from the water of Ayr stone, sand or emery must be thoroughly cleansed off with a stiff brush, detergent and hot running water.

POLISHING MATERIALS

Tripoli   This is used for polishing many different metals. It gives a smooth polished surface, and is used for the first stage of polishing. It occurs in deposits of silica, is mixed with grease, is brown in colour and comes in bars.

Pink porthos   This can be used for polishing silver, but it is more often used for gold. It is a cleaner polish to use

168 Brushing the inside of a goblet with a Turk's head brush

than tripoli, and is harder, so does not spatter as much when applied to the mop. It also polishes steel. Pale pink in colour, it comes in bars.

Rouge This is available in a number of shades of red showing different grades from fine to extra fine. It is used for the second stage of polishing called colouring, and imparts a highly reflective polish on the surface of the metal, a 'black finish'. It is made from red iron oxide powder, bonded with grease and stearic acid, and comes in bar or powder form.

Buff-sticks These are wooden sticks of different sections, with different materials glued to, or wrapped around them depending on their use. Fine polishing papers are glued to, or wrapped around them depending on their use. Fine polishing papers are glued to them as well as leather for use with tripoli or rouge.

Mops These are made from layers of calico or cotton held together by leather washers with a hole through the centre to fit on to the spindle of the polishing motor. Hard calico mops are used with tripoli or pink porthos for the first stage of polishing. Softer calico mops are also used with tripoli or pink porthos and radio rouge, the coarsest rouge.

Soft cotton mops are used with radio rouge, the finer rouges and whiting powder. Every polish, even the different rouges, has separate mops. After every stage of finishing, the metal must be completely cleaned of the compound used. The smallest particle of a different compound on a mop will spoil that mop and take the polishing back a stage. For largework, mops between 10 cm and 15 cm in diameter are used. For a large, plain, round bowl the width is between 1.5 cm and 3 cm; for a straight-sided beaker, a mop 20 cm in diameter can be used.

Felts   These are used on very flat surfaces such as the faces of wires. If they fit the shape of the piece correctly they will impart a good polish to the metal. They come in many shapes and sizes. Used with tripoli, pink porthos and rouge.

Brushes   These are made from hogs' hair, horse hair, fibre or nylon and come in several shapes and sizes and degrees of hardness. They are flexible and so can be used to polish irregular surfaces, but if used without care they can easily smooth off edges. Brushes for the inside of goblets, etc. are called 'Turk's head' brushes. Used with tripoli, pink porthos and rouge.

Woollen mops   Can be used also for the final finish.

Selvyt cloth   A soft flannel-like cloth, it should be kept in the workshop for cleaning metal that has already been polished and may bear finger-marks or a slight tarnish.

Fine cotton gloves   These can be bought from a chemist to handle silver that has been polished when screwing parts together or riveting. Touching newly polished silver with the hands will leave greasy marks and small scratches that show up very clearly. But once silver has been handled it acquires tiny scratches all over which soften and enhance the appearance of the metal.

Various hand brushes   For cleaning the metal after it has been polished. After the grinding process a hard brush is used, but after polishing much softer ones must be used or the surface polish will become scratched. They should always be cleaned well after use.

Boxwood sawdust   This is kept clean in a box near the sink, and when the piece has been brushed with detergent and water it is pushed into the boxwood and left to dry.

POLISHING

By hand   Polishing is only occasionally done by hand, if the piece is flat and the polisher has not had enough experience with the polishing motor. It is a time-consuming process. Once the piece has been rubbed with polishing papers, it is buffed with buff-sticks. These are used in the same way as hand files, having first been rubbed with a polishing compound (tripoli or pink porthos). Once these finer scratches left by the polishing compound have been removed, the work is cleaned with a soft brush and washing-up liquid, and another buff-stick is used, this time charged with rouge. The piece is

169 Polishing with a mop

then lightly finished with a rouge mop on the polishing motor.

By machine   The first stage of polishing, is done with a hard calico mop on the machine. The tripoli or pink porthos is applied to the face of the mop and the metal is moved across the mop, first from one side, then from the other, overlapping the strokes and moving the work continually. As the polish dries up on the mop, more is added. The whole piece will take on a dull shine. As the work progresses the piece is rubbed with a cloth to remove the polish and the surface inspected for scratches and firestain. If any deep firestain does remain, it should be taken off with water of Ayr stone or sand. The metal around the firestain is softer than the firestain and when polished the softer metal will be cut quicker than the other, leaving an uneven surface.

The mop is moved across the scratches, rather than along them as this would cause them to deepen into grooves. If the mop becomes caked with polish a wheel rake or an old hacksaw blade can be run through the polishing face to clear it. If the caking is too solid, the mop should be soaked in hot water, liquid detergent and amonia and left over-night.

The size of the mops used varies according to the work. The larger the mop the greater will be its speed and a large mop should only be used on larger pieces of work. The mop must fit the contours of the work and not be too large to manoeuvre over it or to catch the edges that may jut out. If the mop is too small, especially where felts are being used, it will cut grooves into the metal.

Pressure is applied to the mop for the polish to be effective; the cut of the polish on the metal must be felt, but too much pressure can cause the metal to expand through over-heating, distorting the work, and cause the polish to bind or burn into the surface of the metal. If the

170 Using a felt

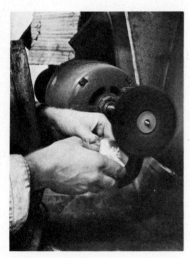

171 Final rouge polish

latter should happen with tripoli or pink porthos, it can be removed with paraffin. With rouge, methylated spirits or paraffin will be effective in some cases, but if it is burnt in, then it must be taken out with water of Ayr stone.

On largework the strokes used should overlap in long sweeps; on smallwork they should cross each other, changing the direction in which the wheel passes over the metal to achieve a uniform finish. Once the first stage of polishing is done, the metal is cleaned and a calico mop with radio rouge is used, again the strokes going across the marks.

The final polish is done with a soft cotton mop, rouge and also paraffin to stop the build-up of rouge on the surface of the metal or the mop, and thus prevent hard lumps from forming on the mop and scratching the metal. This mop will leave a fine film of paraffin on the job and so an old soft cotton mop is run over it. This should be one that has been well impregnated with rouge dust so no new rouge should be added.

This final process gives the black finish which is highly reflective. It is at this time that any further finishing is done to the metal, such as texturing or brass-brushing.

Polishing the insides of boxes is difficult so they are often lined or sand-blasted and gilded to avoid the problem. The metal can be polished before the piece is made up to eliminate some of the marks, but it will still have to be stoned by hand and polished, using very small mops, brushes and felts. A pendant drill used with polishing attachments can often be used for this type of work. It should not be employed on larger pieces to reach into sharp angles, i.e. where a foot-wire joins a bowl, as this is likely to make a groove in the metal.

Burnishing

The principle of burnishing is to compress the metal, giving it a highly reflective polish. A whole piece of work can be burnished but often it is only parts of the piece, such as the inside of a wire or pierced work where polishing on a spindle would be impossible. It is also used if the metal becomes scratched when fitting, riveting or screwing parts together.

The steel used must be brightly polished with no flaws or scratches. It should fit the contours of the work being burnished and have softened edges so as not to scratch the precious metal. The burnishing is done by rubbing the tool over the surface of the metal in parallel, overlapping strokes. It must be lubricated in some way. Saliva is a good medium. The entire surface is worked on slowly, a section at a time, and the marks are then covered by moving across them in parallel lines in the same fashion. The surface must be absolutely free from dirt. The haematite burnishers can be used after this to finish the piece but often the polishing motor is used with a soft mop and rouge to achieve a bright black finish.

172 Pendant drill

173 Silver bowl with frosted finish. Lindsey Middleton, 1979

174 A set of silver candlesticks with textured stems. Gerald Benney, c. 1970

13 Different finishes

A piece of work with the bright, reflective surface typical of a black finish will take on fine scratches all over when it is handled, and with use it will slowly become a softer whiter colour. There are various different ways of finishing the metal after it has been brought to this stage. Whiting powder, powdered chalk, can be applied to the job by mixing with water to a thick paste. The piece is then polished with a soft cotton mop on the polishing motor. This tones down the shine on the metal leaving a soft white sheen on silver, a buttery sheen on gold.

A brass brush used on a polishing motor will leave an even, shiny satin finish on the metal. The brush must be kept well lubricated with washing-up liquid and water, or the brass will bind on the surface of the precious metal, leaving patches of brass. Pumice powder and water rubbed on the job and brushed with a brass brush will leave a dull satin finish.

A fine steel brush will leave an even, fine textured surface, similar to that left by sand-blasting. For a brass or steel brush finish to be successful, all deep marks must be removed from the precious metal. A piece brushed with a brass brush will take on a very bright satin finish if it has first been brought up to a black finish, although if heavy scratches have been left on its surface they will show very clearly; if the piece has not first been brought up to a black finish, heavy scratches will be less noticeable but the piece will be much duller.

There are several other finishes that can be given to the metal by hand. A 'Georgian Butler' finish is achieved by applying whiting powder and water on a soft brush, washing the piece and finally rubbing it with a clean Selvyt cloth. Hand-brushing with whiting and water, and then buffing with a soft cotton mop will produce a 'Victorian Butler' finish. The piece is then washed and lightly polished with a soft mop and rouge. A 'Bright Butler' finish is obtained by rubbing the finished piece with a mixture of rouge powder and water applied with the heel of the hand; the piece is then rubbed with a Selvyt cloth.

175 Silver boxes with textured surfaces done with a pendant drill, and with gold enamelled leaves. Karina Payne, 1978

Texturing

This can be achieved in several ways. Sand-blasting will give the metal a light, even dull texture. It will not obliterate deep scratches, but will cover lighter ones. Glass-shot must be used, not carborundum, which cuts the metal and leaves a grey, absorbent surface. The glass-shot hammers the surface rather than cutting it. Surfaces that are not to be completely sand-blasted should be masked off in some way, for instance, by using Sellotape or something similar.

Dental burrs are used in the pendant drill to give texture. They are available in many shapes and sizes, giving heavy, light and even very fine textures. The heavier ones leave a rough surface that will cover anything except large pin-holes; the lighter ones will not cover pin-holes at all, but will cover light scratches. The better the surface, the more even and predictable will be the texture. If a fine burr is applied to a highly reflective surface the texture will have more sparkle.

Texture can also be obtained by hammering. The face of the hammer is textured in some way, either by filed grooves, or some sort of pattern cut into its surface. The finish on the metal before texturing depends on the finish that is eventually required. The hammering can be done after sanding. The surface of the texture will also depend on whether the texture on the hammer is highly polished or dull. The hammering is done in the same way as planishing, the tool on the inside of the job, fitting it well.

Etching

If only parts of the surface are to be etched the whole is brought up to a black finish and the appropriate parts masked off with an acid resist. If the whole piece is to be etched it need not be brought up to a black finish.

Nitric acid used cold and ferric oxide used hot both give good results when etching silver. Gold can only be etched with aqua regia (nitric and hydrochloric acids). Ferric oxide produces a smooth texture, rather like that produced by sand-blasting. Nitric acid may produce various textures depending on the strength of the acid used. A heavy but smooth texture is achieved if acid and water are mixed (always add the acid to the water), one part acid to three parts water. The acid rounds off corners, giving an even, 'eroded' texture rather than a cut one. Nitric acid used undiluted will work very quickly, so it must be watched continually. It gives a lace-like texture.

Cleaning precious metals

A Selvyt cloth should be used to remove tarnish and fingermarks from a finished piece, which should be

176 Fitzwilliam Cup. This was raised
and the sides then hammered flat.
Jocelyn Burton, 1971

breathed on and rubbed with the cloth. If the tarnish is
too heavy to remove in this way, washing-up liquid with
a few drops of ammonia should be put into a bowl and
hot water poured on top of them. The object is then
soaked in this for a short time, rinsed and dried with a soft
cloth, before being rubbed with the Selvyt cloth. If the
tarnish is very heavy, the piece should be cleaned with a
proprietary brand metal cleaner.

Appendices

TABLES AND DATA

CONVERSION TABLE

To convert	to	multiply by	reciprocal
Weight			
oz troy	g	31.1035	0.03215
oz avoir	g	28.3495	0.03527
oz troy	oz avoir	1.09714	0.9115
1b avoir	kg	0.4536	2.2046
Length			
in	mm	25.4	0.03937
in	cm	2.54	0.3937
in	m	0.0254	39.37
ft	m	0.3048	3.28084
Area			
in²	mm²	645.16	0.00155
in²	cm²	6.4516	0.1550
Volume			
in³	cm³	16.3871	0.061024

APPROXIMATE WEIGHT PER SQUARE INCH OF SHEET AND PER FOOT OF
ROUND WIRE OF METALS AND ALLOYS

In the table below specific gravity figures for a number of
metals and alloys are listed, and in the next table factors
are given covering a range of thicknesses of sheet and
diameters of round wire.

To find the approximate weight in grammes of a
square inch of sheet or a foot length of round wire,
multiply the specific gravity figure of the metal or alloy
by the appropriate thickness or diameter factor.

For example:

Weight of one square inch of 9 carat DF sheet 0.55 in
thick is 11.2 × 0.9 = 10.08 grammes.

Weight of one foot of 18 carat HB wire 0.039 in
diameter is 15.7 × 0.23 = 3.61 grammes.

Pure platinum ....21.4   18 carat SW 16.6
97% platinum 20.6
                                    14 carat HB 14.1
Pure palladium ....12.0   14 carat JP 13.8
3% molybdenum-   14 carat AF 13.0
palladium ....12.0   14 carat WA 13.5
                                    14 carat M 13.2
Fine silver ....10.5   14 carat DR 13.3
Britannia silver ....10.5   14 carat MW 12.9
Standard silver ....10.3   14 carat SW 14.6
830 Q silver 10.2
                                    9 carat P 11.3
Fine gold ....19.3   9 carat BY 12.4
                                    9 carat DF 11.2
22 carat DS ....17.8   9 carat C 11.2
22 carat R ....17.7   9 carat SC 11.1
                                    9 carat G 11.0
18 carat HB ....15.7   9 carat BR 11.4
18 carat FG ....15.9   9 carat MR 11.2
18 carat AK ....15.1   9 carat HW 11.0
18 carat MR ....15.2   9 carat MW 12.6
18 carat FW ....14.7   9 carat SW 12.8
18 carat MW 16.4

FACTORS FOR SHEET

Thickness

inch	.000	.001	.002	.003	.004	.005	.006	.007	.008	.009
.000		.016	.033	.049	.006	.082	.098	.11	.13	.15
.010	.16	.18	.20	.21	.23	.25	.26	.28	.29	.31
.020	.33	.34	.36	.38	.39	.41	.43	.44	.46	.48
.030	.49	.51	.52	.54	.56	.57	.59	.61	.62	.64
.040	.66	.67	.69	.70	.72	.74	.75	.77	.79	.80
.050	.82	.84	.85	.87	.88	.90	.92	.93	.95	.97
.060	.98	.99	1.02	1.03	1.05	1.06	1.08	1.10	1.11	1.13
.070	1.15	1.16	1.18	1.20	1.21	1.23	1.24	1.26	1.28	1.29
.080	1.31	1.33	1.34	1.36	1.38	1.39	1.41	1.42	1.44	1.46
.090	1.47	1.49	1.51	1.52	1.54	1.56	1.57	1.59	1.60	1.62

FACTORS FOR WIRE

Diameter

inch	.000	.001	.002	.003	.004	.005	.006	.007	.008	.009
.000			.001	.002	.004	.006	.008	.010	.013	
.010	.015	.019	.022	.026	.030	.035	.039	.045	.050	.056
.020	.062	.068	.074	.082	.089	.096	.10	.11	.12	.13
.030	.14	.15	.16	.17	.18	.19	.20	.21	.22	.23
.040	.25	.26	.27	.28	.30	.31	.33	.34	.36	.37
.050	.38	.40	.42	.43	.45	.47	.48	.50	.52	.54
.060	.56	.57	.59	.61	.63	.65	.67	.69	.71	.73
.070	.76	.78	.80	.82	.84	.87	.89	.91	.94	.96
.080	.99	1.01	1.04	1.06	1.09	1.12	1.14	1.16	1.19	1.22
.090	1.25	1.28	1.30	1.33	1.36	1.39	1.42	1.45	1.48	1.51

Thickness	.40 mm	.50 mm	.55 mm	.60 mm	.70 mm	.80 mm
approximate equivalent {	.016 in *G6	.019 in G7	.0215 in G8	.024 in G9	.028 in G10	.032 in G11
Diameter of circle, inch						
2	8.3	10.4	11.5	12.5	14.6	16.7
$2\frac{1}{4}$	10.6	13.2	14.5	15.8	18.5	21.1
$2\frac{1}{2}$	13.0	16.3	17.9	19.6	22.8	26.1
$2\frac{3}{4}$	15.8	19.7	21.7	23.7	27.6	31.6
3	18.8	23.5	25.8	28.2	32.9	37.6
$3\frac{1}{4}$	22.0	27.6	30.3	33.1	38.6	44.1
$3\frac{1}{2}$	25.6	32.0	35.2	38.4	44.7	51.1
$3\frac{3}{4}$	29.4	36.7	40.4	44.0	51.4	58.7
4	33.4	41.7	45.9	50.1	58.4	66.8
$4\frac{1}{2}$	42.3	52.8	58.1	63.4	74.0	84.5
5	52.2	65.2	71.7	78.3	91.3	104
$5\frac{1}{2}$	63.1	78.9	86.8	94.7	110	126
6	75.1	93.9	103	113	131	150
$6\frac{1}{2}$	88.2	110	121	132	154	176
7	102	128	141	153	179	205
$7\frac{1}{2}$	117	147	161	176	205	235
8	134	167	184	200	234	267
$8\frac{1}{2}$	151	189	207	226	264	302
9	169	211	232	254	296	338
$9\frac{1}{2}$	188	235	259	283	330	377
10	209	261	287	313	365	417
$10\frac{1}{2}$	230	288	316	345	403	460
11	253	316	347	379	442	505
$11\frac{1}{2}$	276	345	380	414	483	552
12	301	376	413	451	526	601
$12\frac{1}{2}$	326	408	448	489	571	652
13	353	441	485	529	617	705
$13\frac{1}{2}$	380	475	523	571	666	761
14	409	511	563	614	716	818
$14\frac{1}{2}$	439	549	603	658	768	878
15	470	587	646	704	822	939
$15\frac{1}{2}$	501	627	690	752	878	1000
16	534	668	735	801	935	1070
17	603	754	829	905	1060	1210
18	676	845	930	1010	1180	1350
19	753	942	1040	1130	1320	1510
20	835	1040	1150	1250	1460	1670

* Birmingham Metal Gauge (Shakespeare's)

.90 mm	.95 mm	1.10 mm	1.20 mm	1.30 mm	1.50 mm	1.65 mm
.036 in	.038 in	.043 in	.048 in	.051 in	.059 in	.065 in
G13	G14	G15	G16	G18	G20	G12
18.8	19.8	23.0	25.0	27.1	31.3	34.4
23.8	25.1	29.1	31.7	34.3	39.6	43.6
29.4	31.0	35.9	39.1	42.4	48.9	53.8
35.5	37.5	43.4	47.4	51.3	59.2	65.1
42.3	44.6	51.7	56.4	61.1	70.4	77.5
49.6	52.4	60.6	66.1	71.7	82.7	90.9
57.5	60.7	70.3	76.7	83.1	95.9	105
66.0	69.7	80.7	88.1	95.4	110	121
75.1	79.3	91.8	100	109	125	138
95.1	100	116	127	137	158	174
117	124	143	157	170	196	215
142	150	174	189	205	237	260
169	178	207	225	244	282	310
198	209	243	265	287	331	364
230	243	281	307	332	384	422
264	279	323	352	382	440	484
301	317	367	401	434	501	551
339	358	415	452	490	566	622
380	402	465	507	549	634	697
424	447	518	565	612	706	777
470	496	574	626	678	783	861
518	547	633	690	748	863	949
568	600	695	758	821	947	1040
621	656	759	828	897	1040	1140
676	714	827	9P2	977	1130	1240
734	775	897	978	1060	1220	1350
794	838	970	1060	1150	1320	1460
856	903	1050	1140	1240	1430	1570
920	972	1130	1230	1330	1530	1690
987	1040	1210	1320	1430	1650	1810
1060	1120	1290	1410	1530	1760	1940
1130	1190	1380	1500	1630	1880	2070
1200	1270	1470	1600	1740	2000	2200
1360	1430	1660	1810	1960	2260	2490
1520	1610	1860	2030	2200	2540	2790
1700	1790	2070	2260	2450	2830	3110
1880	1980	2300	2500	2710	3130	3440

BRITISH ASSOCIATION THREAD (B.A.)

Tap size	Tapping drill size (mm)	Clearance drill size (mm)
0	5.10	6.10
1	4.50	5.40
2	4.00	4.80
3	3.40	4.20
4	3.00	3.70
5	2.65	3.30
6	2.30	2.90
7	2.05	2.60
8	1.80	2.25
9	1.55	1.95
10	1.40	1.75
11	1.20	1.60
12	1.05	1.40
13	0.98	1.30
14	0.80	1.10
15	0.70	0.98
16	0.60	0.88

ASSAY OFFICES

The Assay Office
The Goldsmiths' Hall
Gutter Lane
London EC2

The Assay Office
New Hall Street
Birmingham B11SB

The Assay Office
137 Portobello Street
Sheffield S14DR

The Assay Office
The Goldsmiths' Hall
15 Queens Street
Edinburgh

The Assay Office
Dublin Castle
Dublin
Eire

SUPPLIERS

Precious metals

Advance Findings Co.
Diamond House
36 Hatton Gardens
London EC1

J. Blundell & Sons Ltd
199 Wardour Street
London W1

The Sheffield Smelting
   Co. Ltd
132 St John Street
London EC1

Johnson Matthey Group
in England:
Johnson Matthey Metals
   Ltd
43 Hatton Garden
London EC1

Johnson Matthey Metals
   Ltd
Vittoria Street
Birmingham

Johnson Matthey Metals
   Ltd
173–5 Arundel Gate
Sheffield

in the USA:

Johnson Matthey Inc.
608 Fifth Avenue,
New York, NY 10020

Matthey Bishop Inc.
Malvern, PA 19355

Copper, brass, gilding metal, etc.

J. Smith & Sons
   (Clerkenwell) Ltd
50 St John's Square
London EC1

Tantalum and niobium

Elvants Ltd
Sinclair House
The Avenue
London W13

Tool steel

Macreadys Metals Co.
    Ltd
Pentonville Road
London N1

Casting equipment

V. N. Barrett (Sales) Ltd
1 Mayo Road
Croydon
Surrey

Hoben Davies Ltd
Spencroft Road
Holditch Industrial Estate
Newcastle-under-Lyme
Staffs.

Hydebourne Ltd
46 Rainham Road
London NW10

Jewellery and dental waxes

Claudius Ash
Summit House
Moon Lane
Barnet
Herts.

Cottrell & Co.
15 Charlotte Street
London W1

Materials for sand casting

Berk Ltd
8 Baker Street
London W1
(Wyoming bentonite)

British Industrial Sands
    Ltd
Wray Common
Reigate
Surrey
(Ryarsh sand)

Corn Products Ltd
Area Sales Office
Epsom
Surrey
(Kordek C1205 or any
    cereal binder)

Polishing materials and acids

T. A. Hutchinson Ltd
16 St John's Lane
London EC1

Glass linings

in England:

S. W. Aldridge,
Elizabethan Works
2 Ivy Road
London E17

in the USA:

Blue Glass Company
6501 Lake Washington
    Boulevard NE
Apartment C
Kirkland, Washington
    98033

Silversmiths' tools

C. Cooper
23 Hatton Wall
London EC1

F. Pike
589 Hatton Gardens
London EC1

C. V. Salvo Ltd
88 Hatton Gardens
London EC1

H. S. Walsh
12 Clerkenwell Road
London EC1

Engineers' tools

Buck and Ryan
101 Tottenham Court
    Road, London W1

C. H. Fowler & Co. Ltd
15 Greville Street
London EC1
(also stock tool steel)

S. Tyzack & Son Ltd
341 Old Street
London EC1

Tool suppliers in the USA

Allcraft Tool and Supply
    Co. Inc.
100 Frank Road
Hicksville, NY 11801

Contenti Supply Co. Inc.
55 Rice Street
Providence, RI 02907

C. R. Hill Co.
2734, W. Eleven Mile
    Road
Berkeley, MI 48072

Dick Ellis Co.
908 Venice Boulevard
Los Angeles, CA 90015

Friedheim Tool Supply
    Co. Inc.
412 West Sixth Street
Los Angeles, CA 90014

Gamzon Bros Inc.
21 West 46th Street
New York, NY 10036

Paul H. Gesswein and Co.
    Inc.
255 Hancock Avenue
Bridgeport, CT 06605

William Dixon Co.
750 Washington Avenue
Carlstadt, NJ 07072

Brass and bronze castings

P. Wilkinson
115 Bramley Road
Ladbroke Grove
London W10

Bibliography

STATON ABBEY, *The Goldsmiths' and Silversmiths' Handbook*, London 1952

GEORGE BLACHFORD, *Metalwork in Theory and Practice*, London 1958

BERNARD CUZNER, *A Silversmith's Manual*, London 1935

ALEXANDER DEL MAR, *A History of the Precious Metals from the earliest times to the present*, London 1885

ROBERT GOODDEN and PHILIP POPHAM, *Silversmithing*, London and New York 1971

DENYS HAY, *The Italian Renaissance in its Historical Background*, Cambridge 1961

GEOFFREY HOLDEN, *The Craft of the Silversmith*, London and New York 1954

HERBERT MARYON, *Metalwork and Enamelling*, 4th edition, revised, London 1959

STUART PIGGOTT, *The Dawn of Civilization*, London and New York 1961

DUNSTAN PRUDEN, *Silversmithing*, London 1933

T. A. RICKARD, *Man and Metals*, London and New York 1932

ERNEST A. SMITH, *The Sampling and the Assay of Precious Metals*, London 1913

——, *Working in Precious Metals*, London 1933; reissued in facsimile 1978

KEITH SMITH, *Practical Silversmithing*, London 1975

GERALD TAYLOR, *Silver*, Harmondsworth 1956

OPPI UNTRACHT, *Metal Techniques for Craftsmen*, Garden City, N.Y. 1968; London 1969

HENRY WILSON, *Silverwork and Jewellery*, 1903

Periodicals

J. S. FORBES, 'Hallmarking of Gold, Silver and Platinum', *The Metallurgist and Materials Technologist*, London, March 1975

P. E. GAINSBURY, 'Miracles are Expensive', *British Jeweller*, Birmingham, February 1969

——, 'Jewellery Investment Casting Machines', *Gold Bulletin*, Johannesburg, January 1979

Johnson Matthey Metals, Ltd, *Investment Casting* (data sheet from their catalogue), London

——, *Products and Services for the Manufacturer in Precious Metals* (data sheet from their catalogue), London

Reports of the Worshipful Company of Goldsmiths Technical Advisory Committee, T.A.C. Project Report Nos 4a/2, 1a/1, 1b/1, 1b/2, 1b/4/s, 1b/5, London

Index

Page numbers in italics refer to illustrations